As Per FYUGP Syllabus (NEP)

ADVERTISEMENT MANAGEMENT

[For B.Com. 2nd Semester Students of Dibrugarh University, Assam and other Universities of North-East India]

SARITA ARORA
M.Com., MBA, M.Phil.
Assistant Professor
Sri Aurobindo College of Commerce and Management
LUDHIANA

PRERNA AHUJA
M.Com., UGC–NET
Assistant Professor
Sri Aurobindo College of Commerce and Management
LUDHIANA

KALYANI PUBLISHERS

LUDHIANA – NEW DELHI – NOIDA (U.P.) – HYDERABAD – CHENNAI
KOLKATA – CUTTACK – GUWAHATI – KOCHI – BENGALURU

KALYANI PUBLISHERS

Head Office

B-3251/B, Street No. 5, Backside Sandhu Tower, Gurdev Nagar, **Ludhiana-**141 001 • Ph : 0161-2760031
E-mail : kalyanibooks@yahoo.co.in **Website :** www.kalyanipublishers.co.in

Administration Office

4779/23, Ansari Road, Daryaganj, **New Delhi**-110 002 • Ph : 011-23271469, 23274393
E-mail : kalyani_delhi@kalyanipublishers.in

Works

B-16, Sector-8, **NOIDA** (U.P.)

Branches

1, Mahalakshmi Street, T. Nagar, **Chennai-**600 017 • Ph : 044-24344684
Gopabandhu Lane, Behind Govt. Bus Stand, Badambadi, **Cuttack-**753 012 (Odisha) • Ph : 0671-2311391
4-3-65/2/A, Behind HVS Public School, Raghunath Bagh
Sultan Bazar, **Hyderabad-**500 095 • Ph : 040-24750368
10/2B, Ramanath Mazumdar Street, **Kolkata-**700 009 • Ph : 033-22416024
Arunalaya, 1st Floor, Saraswati Road, Pan Bazar, **Guwahati-**781 001 • Ph : 0361-2731274
Koratti Parambil House, Convent Road, **Kochi-**682 035 • Ph : 0484-2367189
No. 24 & 25, 1st Floor, Hameed Shah Complex, Cubbonpet Main Road, **Bengaluru-**560 002

T 39795 07
U-42375 05

8 + 192 = 200 Pages 20" x 30" 25 Forms

Reprinted. 2025

Gautam Graphic Printers
(MISC–24–ADV-MGT-DB)

PRINTED IN INDIA

Thakur Enterprises
D-31, Sector 4, Bawana, Delhi-110039

Preface

In the dynamic realm of business, where markets evolve and consumer behaviours shape the landscape, the role of advertising stands as a linchpin in connecting products with people. Advertising is not just about creating catchy slogans or eye-catching visuals; it's a strategic discipline that requires a deep understanding of consumer behaviour, market trends, and the power of communication. This book serves as a guide through the fascinating landscape of advertising, offering insights, strategies, and practical tools to navigate the challenges of this dynamic field.

This book intends to be your go-to resource, to enhance your knowledge about the subject of Advertising Management and also helps students to understand the intricacies associated with this subject. The chapters are designed in such a way that student gets thorough knowledge of the foundations of Advertising, the decisions related to segmentation, positioning, methods that must be used for the advertising messaging, and media selection for advertising. An attempt is made to make subject more understandable as real-world examples and case studies are incorporated to bridge the gap between theory and application.

We, the authors are highly thankful and obliged to Mr. Tarun, ***Kalyani Publishers*** and their entire team for taking all the pains and efforts for publishing this book. We are grateful to our family, friends and colleagues who inspired and encouraged us to work for this book.

2024

SARITA ARORA

PRERNA AHUJA

Syllabus

DIBRUGARH UNIVERSITY

As Per [NEP] (FYUG) Syllabus

Semester-II

Title of the Course : Advertising Management

Course Code : MINCOM2

Nature of the Course : Minor

Course Credit : 04 Credits

Distribution of Marks : 80 (End Sem) + 20 (In-Sem)

Objective :

To acquaint the students with the meaning of Advertising and its planning as well as Decision Making for the selection of the target market, segmentation, media as well as the creative contents.

UNITS	COURSE CONTENTS	L	T	P
I FOUNDATION OF ADVERTISING *(20 Marks)*	Field of Advertising (Advertiser, Facilitating, Institutions, Perspectives on Advertising) Advertising Planning (Framework, Situation Analysis, Marketing Plan) Decision Making in Advertising (Persuasion) Process, Facilitating Agencies.	12	02	–
II OBJECTIVE SETTING AND POSITIONING *(20 Marks)*	Integrated Marketing Communication (Sales Promotion, Action-oriented Communication, Public Relations, Integrating the Different Elements) Setting Goals and Objectives (Behavioural Dynamics, DAGMAR Approach, Specifying the Target Segment) Segmentation and Positioning (Determinants, Strategies for Segmentation and Position, Decision-making)	14	02	–
III MESSAGE STRATEGY *(20 Marks)*	Attention and Comprehension (Recall Comprehension, and Interpretation) Understanding Benefit based Attitude (level) and Components, Attributes, Multi-attribute Models (2 nos.) Word-of-mouth Advertising	14	02	–

IV MEDIA STRATEGY *(20 Marks)*	Art of Copy Writing (Illustrating, Layout, Types of Commercials, Creative Styles) 6- II III Setting Media Budget Economic Analysis, Market Experimentation and Budgeting, Regression Analysis for Budgeting) Media Tactics (Media Class, Vehicles, Option decisions)	**12**	**02**	**–**
	TOTAL	**52**	**08**	**–**

Where, L = Lectures, T=Tutorials, P = Practicals

Modes of In-Semester Assessment : ***(20 Marks)***

- One Sessional Examination 10 Marks
- Other (any of the following listed below) 10 Marks
    - Group Discussion
    - Assignment
    - Seminar Presentation on any of the relevant topics
    - Hands-on-learning

Contents

Chapter 1

FIELD OF ADVERTISING

INTRODUCTION

Advertising is all over the place, on TV and radio, in newspapers and magazines, on billboards and even plastered across the sides of buses. It is persistent and persuasive and nearly everyone in the modern world is influenced by some degree of advertising. It has formed an integral part of our social and economic systems. In our complex society, it has evolved into a vital communications system for both consumers as well as businesses. ***Advertising is the fuel of enterprise.*** It not only creates awareness about the products or services, but also persuades us to think in a certain way. The global market has expanded manifold in the last few decades and countless products are being launched almost every day. The companies are engaged in cutthroat competition to accentuate their products.

It was in the 1970's that an advertisement appeared for the first time in Indian print media in Hickey's Bengal Gazette. Indian advertising, since then, has evolved, reflecting the change that the country's economy as well as society has undergone. Presently, there are a lot of advertising agencies in this billion-dollar industry who recognize different opportunities' methods for contacting and persuading current and prospective customers.

DEFINITION

Advertising is any paid form of non-personal presentation and promotion of goods, services, or ideas by an identified sponsor. – **Philip Kotler**

Advertising is a printed, written, oral and illustrated art of selling. Its objective is to encourage sales of the advertiser's products and to create in the mind of people, individually or collectively, an impression in favor of the advertiser's interest.

–Frank Presbrey

Advertising consists of all activities involved in presenting to a group a non-personal, oral, or visual, openly sponsored identified message regarding a product, service, or idea. The message, called an advertisement, is disseminated through one or more media, and is paid for by the identified sponsor. **–William stanton**

Advertising is salesmanship in print. **–John E. Kennedy**

Advertising means any paid form of non-personal presentation and promotion of ideas, goods, or services by an identified sponsor.

–American Marketing Association (AMA)

FEATURES AND FUNCTIONS OF ADVERTISING

Advertising is the non-personal communication of information usually paid for and usually persuasive in nature about products, service or ideas by an identified sponsor through the various media. **-Bovee (1992, 7)**

1. NON-PERSONAL

There are two ways to sell any product or service: personally, and non-personally. Personal selling requires the seller and the buyer to be in direct contact and they have various advantages and disadvantages as discussed below:

Some of the advantages are:

- The seller has the time to discuss the product in detail and clarify any psychological or logical objection which the buyer might have.
- The seller can see if the message is getting across to the buyer. If the customer is bored or yawns, the seller can change the approach towards the buyer.

Some of the disadvantages are:

- As far as cost is concerned, personal selling is labor intensive and deals with only one buyer at a time.
- It is time consuming. Selling a water purifier or a car can take days, and no one has time to wait in this fast-moving world.

Advertising is basically a replacement of personal selling. There are several advantages of this:

- Advertisements can create awareness through various sources like print, broadcast or even the internet.

- the message is based on thorough research of the potential customers, their preferences, their buying behavior, message elements that influence them etc.
- Advertising is far cheaper per potential customer than personal selling. Advertising deals with millions of customers at a time unlike personal selling which deals with one customer at a time.

2. COMMUNICATION

It is a process by which information, ideas, feelings can be passed through speech or pictures. Communication uses all the five senses: smell, touch, taste, sound and sight. However, only two are useful in advertising - **sound** and **sight**.

• Sound

It can be used in a variety of media, from radio to television to any new technology to present the sales message. It is also capable of presenting words and creating a vivid imagery in the minds of the consumers.

For example, a beer commercial may play the sounds of a bar in the background, and the listeners may imagine themselves in their own favorite bar and perhaps ordering that brand of beer. Thus, sound in the form of words is quite useful to an advertiser in influencing the customer.

• Sight

Sight is plausibly the most useful of the communication channels available to an advertiser. Through sight, it is possible to use images as well as words effectively. Moreover, it's *better to open the eye than to scratch the ear*. Thus, there is no need to speak words to convey meaning. They can be printed as well. Though it is difficult to create an emotional impact but through spoken words it becomes easy to influence the buyers. For example: a drop of water on mango in the advertisement of Slice may not consciously register "I see there's a drop of water on this mango" but would unconsciously leave an impression of freshness and delicacy.

Thus, sound and sight are of great value and effectiveness.

3. INFORMATION

Information is elucidated as knowledge, facts, or news. However, one should bear in mind that one person's information is another person's scam. Information comes in many forms. It can be complete or incomplete. It can be biased or deceptive.

Complete information reveals all the facts about a product even if it is time consuming. For example, to tell all about Tesla car would require its appearance, manufacturer, what percentage of parts are made in which countries, cost of upkeep, mileage, cost (basic and with all combination of options), sales and excise taxes per state, preparation costs, insurance costs per state and locale, ride characteristics, braking distance at many different speeds, etc. All of this would require a documentary, not an advertisement. Thus, advertisers must provide only information which is useful to the target audience.

Bias means partial towards something, feeling that something is better or worse than other things. In advertising this is necessary as an advertiser is biased towards their own product and against the competition: selling their product is the way they make their money and increase their market share, and as a result competitor's sales reduce. Thus, any advertiser will use words and images that show fantastically exaggerated claims of how good their product is and/or how poor their competition's is. This is biased information, but recognized and accepted by industry consumers and regulators -- it is called **puffery**.

However, sometimes biased information goes beyond legitimate puffery and slips into fraudulent claims, the deliberate use of misleading words and images. In other words, lying to the customer about the quality of a product. Such claims are illegal.

4. PAID FOR

". . . Paid for . . . "isstraightforward. Advertising is not free of cost. Advertisers, known as sponsors, spend financial resources preparing messages, buying media, and monitoring advertising efforts. It is the costliest option for promotion as the company prepares its advertising budget to appropriate the advertising costs.

5. PERSUASIVE

"Persuasive" means inducing to do something through reasoning. The basic purpose of advertising is to identify and differentiate one product from another to create a preference of the product in the mind of the consumer.

6. PRODUCTS, SERVICES, OR IDEAS

Products, services, or ideas are the things that are refined for sale.

For example, If the function of a car, transportation, is all that is important, then manufacturers would need only build motorized boxes on wheels, and consumers would be happy with them. However, that is not the case: as nowadays the number of models and types of cars is huge, and this variety exists due to consumer demand. Maybe the value is social as the type of car a person drives is often indicative of that person's social status. Driving a BMW is termed as 'cool' as to driving a Volvo or a Toyota. Maybe the value is psychological. Some cars may make a person feel secure or give them self-esteem or ownership. Or maybe the value is economic. Some cars may be cheaper to run, give better mileage, or cause less damage to the environment.

The above four values, functional, social, psychological, and economic, determine whether he/she will buy that product or not. Companies, through research, try to determine what values consumers want in their products, and then advertise to show how their product satisfies the customers' bundle of values by differentiating with competitors' product. There are three basic differentiations: perceptible, imperceptible, and induced.

- **Perceptible**

Perceptible differences are those that differentiate between the products of the same product class. The consumer can easily see that a Hyundai car is different from Honda car. Perceptible differences allow a person to make an instant recognition of one product as opposed to another.

- **Imperceptible**

Imperceptible differences are those that exist between one product and others but are not that obvious. For example, there are imperceptible but ardent differences between CP/M, MS-DOS and Apple, MacIntosh computers. One cannot simply differentiate between the two computers.

- **Induced**

For many products, there is no significant difference between one and another. For many brands of cigarettes, packaged products, liquor, cleansers and soaps, rice, over-the-counter health products, financial products etc., etc., there is essentially no difference between one brand and another. These products are called parity products. For these products, the only way to differentiate one from another is to induce or instigate that difference, to persuade people that there actually is some difference, and that difference is important to them. These differences are created through advertising.

Heidelberg, the working man's beer, Michelob, the sophisticated nightlife beer, Bud, the athletic beer, Miller Lite, the fun and funny beer, Coors, the environmental beer, Coors Light, the fast beer; All of these are images projected onto products that have virtually no difference between them (taste tests show that few people can tell one from the other). Once that difference is firmly established in the target audience's mind, a company can often rely on habit, brand loyalty and/or cognitive dissonance to get repeat business.

7. IDENTIFIED SPONSORS

Identified sponsors means telling the audience who you are. There are two reasons for this: first, it's a legal requirement, and second, it makes good sense.

Legally, an advertiser must identify themselves as the sponsor of an ad so that the customers know who has spent money on the advertisement irrespective of the media utilized. This prevents the audience from getting a misleading idea about the advertisement or its content. For example, many ads that appear in newspapers look like news articles: same appearance, typeface, use of columns, etc. Since it is an ad, somewhere on it there must appear the word "advertisement" to ensure that the audience does not think it is an objective reporting of news.

Second, it makes good sense for a sponsor to identify themselves in the ad. If the sponsor doesn't, it is possible for the audience to believe the ad is for a competitor's product, thus wasting all the time, money and creativity that went into making and placing the ad.

8. VARIOUS MEDIA

Advertisements use non personal form of communication which included various media like newspapers, magazines, radio, television, billboards, transit cards, sandwich boards, skywriting, and posters. The advertisers may use a combination of different media in order to represent the voice of the company.

OBJECTIVES OF ADVERTISING

There are 3 main objectives of advertising. These are:

- **To Inform :** Advertisements are used to create a brand identity in the target market. It informs the potential customers about the brand and its products so as to attain its business goals.
- **To Persuade :** Persuading customers to enact a task is an eminent objective of advertising. The tasks may involve buying or trying the products and services offered, to form a brand image, develop a favorable attitude towards the brand.
- **To Remind :** Advertising helps in reinforcing the brand identity and also, reassures the existing and potential customers about the brand vision. Advertising helps the brand to maintain top of mind awareness and to avoid competitors stealing the customers.

Other objectives of advertising are subsets of these three objectives. These subsets are:

- Brand Building
- Increasing Sales
- Creating Demand
- Engagement
- Expanding Customer Base
- Changing Customers' attitudes, etc.

SCOPE OF ADVERTISING

Under the scope of advertising a marketer must know what activities are included in the scope of advertising and what activities are not included in the scope of advertising.

Activities in the scope of advertising

- Advertising through various media creates awareness about the products' price and other specifications leading to greater sales.
- Helps the intermediaries by promoting the product.
- It builds brand loyalty.
- It builds confidence in the minds of the consumers as well as the businesses.
- Builds goodwill and brand image of the product.
- A good ad campaign helps to expand the market.

Activities not in the scope of advertising

- It includes all those activities which resemble advertising but are not actually advertising.
- All those advertisements with fantastic claims which are designed to deceive the customers.
- Advertisements that have an element of vulgarity in its display
- Advertisements which are aimed at hurting the sentiments of a particular group or evencompetitors.
- Advertisements which have stereotypical claims against a particular group.

DIFFERENCE BETWEEN ADVERTISING AND PERSONAL SELLING

Basis	Advertising	Personal Selling
FORM	Impersonal form of communication	Personal form of communication
REACH	Reaches masses	Limited number of people can be contacted at a particular time

COST	Cost per person is low	Cost per person is very high
MEDIUM	Mass media like TV, radio, newspaper etc.	Makes use of salesperson to contact the buyer
FLEXIBILITY	Inflexible as message cannot be changed according to buyer's needs	Flexible as the salesperson can change his approach according to consumer's needs
TIME	Covers wide market in short time	Takes a lot of time to cover the market
TYPE OF MESSAGE	Standardized message	Flexible approach and message can be changed
FEEDBACK	Lacks direct feedback	Direct and immediate feedback
ROLE	Creates interest of consumer in the firm's product	Helps in decision making by a consumer
UTILITY	Useful to ultimate consumer as it creates awareness about the product	More useful to intermediaries like traders and retailers.

ROLE OF ADVERTISING:

I. Manufacturers and Advertising:

Manufacturers and producers, who intend to make available goods to the people at profit, do take full advantage of advertising as a major weapon to popularize their products and services.The specific benefits that accrue to the manufacturers are:

1. **It sustains and increases the sales turnover:** It is said "Good wine needs no bush". However, in today's competitive world even the best product, needs a medium to create its unique identity. Advertising does this, by changing the customer's perception of the product which thereby leads to increase in sales of the product. Moreover, the rate of turnover once achieved needs to be sustained and increased. This can be achieved by fabricating reminders through advertising. This helps in repeated sales. And an effective, regular and creative advertisement helps in generating a more loyal customer base.

2. **It maintains the existing market and explores the new:** A progressive company always has its eyes on the future business prospects and also, cannot afford to lose sight of the current position. A company's success is reflected not only in creating

market but its maintenance and extension. It is obvious that if an advertising campaign decreases, the products are not measured up to, the consumer expectations. Moreover, many businesses today create a forceful entry in the market and are backed up by claims through advertisement. In such newly exposed markets, advertising does spade-work for the sponsor to sow the seeds of prosperity.

3. **It controls product prices:** Through advertising, it is possible to control the product prices with profit, particularly the retail prices. Very often the greedy retailers exploit the needy consumers by charging higher prices. If this consumer exploitation is not bridled, both the producers as well as the consumers are to suffer. The manufacturer can help him and consumers by printing the maximum retail price on the product packages. Thus, it's an effective way to avoid "price wars" and unfair competition.

II. Middlemen and Advertising:

In the channel of distribution, middlemen act as the essential link between the manufacturers and the consumers. Their existence is justified by the functions they perform and the services they render. Here, benefits of advertising are seen from angle of retailer a last link in the channel of distribution:

1. **It guarantees quick sales:** Every retailer holding the stocks of different producers is interested in quick turnover. Advertising makes the customer aware of the variety of products available in the market and this accelerates the pace of sales. A faster sale reduces dead stock, capital lock-up; overhead expenses and increases the profits. Advertising gives him much flexibility and freedom to better serve the needs of consumers. Therefore, it gives him a chance to earn better by serving better.
2. **It acts as salesman:** As John E. Kennedy claimed, "Advertising is a salesmanship in print." What a travelling salesman does for the firm is done by advertising at least cost and at a quicker pace. That is why; most retail organizations are willing to spend on advertising which attracts consumers to the stores where the counter salesmen cater to their needs. In fact, advertising has been declared as a boon to retailers who are freed from the problems of sales management. In fact, goods are sold at a faster pace by advertising as it creates a favorable impression of the brand in the minds of the consumers.
3. **It makes retail price maintenance possible:** The consumers are very keen on getting quality products at stable price over a longer period. As advertisements include all the necessary information like manufactured and expiry date along with the maximum retail price of the product, the consumers can plan their expenditure by matching it with their budget accordingly. This gives a relief to the consumers as the prices do not vary for at least three months to one year.

III. Salesforce and Advertising:

Personal selling is the personal form of selling, while advertising is non-personal form of selling. Both are important for successful marketing. Both are to be harmonized for the best results.The salesforce stands benefitted as under:

1. **It creates colorful background:** A good salesman is nothing less than an actor who by his expertise in selling wins the hearts of consumers and sells the company products and services. All such sales sharpness has value and the glamour only when he has a matching backdrop. He may be dignified, diplomatic, versatile salesman but the extent of his success rests heavily on the colorful background created by the advertising. Salesmanship without advertising is like a song without music or a whisky without water. Advertising creates stage for him for his acting to stage effects to magnify his performance.

2. **It reduces his burden of job:** Advertising differentiates and creates awareness of the products and services available in the market. It convinces the customers to purchase the product by providing them the necessary information. This reduces the task of the salesman who was forced to play the double role of advertising and salesmanship both rolled into one. As advertising already provides the necessary information, the only task left is closing the deal which is performed by the salesman. Thus, the task of the salesman has become easier and cozier.

3. **It instills self-confidence:** A salesforce that is self-confident and drive-packed is an asset, rather than an army which needs a big push without self-start. Advertising, by educating salesforce, acts a creative force as it instills self-confidence, initiative and drive in them. Advertising gears the salesmen to the top by making those initiators and confident.

IV. Consumers and Advertising:

The final aim of all marketing efforts is to satisfy the needs of consumers by transmitting the benefits of productive efficiency to the final users. Advertising is an essential concomitant of modern marketing mechanism that helps consumers in three ways:

1. **It is a driving-force in decision-making:** The current complicated world of industry and trade has been able to provide with the most attainable varieties of products to such an extent that the consumers are at loss to make up their mind. Further, each manufacturer claims that his products are the best. In this scenario, advertising that comes to the rescue of a consumer to select the best by providing him with comparative account of each in terms of features, prices, utility, quality, durability, convenience and therefore, the consumer finds it easy to decide with such ready information.
2. **It ensures better quality products at reasonable prices:** Advertising stimulates the sales of a good product and accelerates the destruction of bad product or products by engraving the image of the product in the minds of the customers and earns a long-standing reputation for the manufacture. It is the work of branding to build the brand image because; every brand stands for benefits, value, price, promises and its social impact. This means that a customer gets value for the money spent. Maintenance of quality and price of a product is important not only as an objective but as a barometer for quality improvement and price reduction.
3. **It saves great deal of time and effort:** The modern chivalrous living has made the members of the family to put forth their best to make both the ends to meet. In the past, the products were cheaper, and the requirements were limited. Hence, it was enough for a single member to work and earn income for the entire family. However, today's trends have led to inflation and more members have resorted to contribute to the family income. Every single person is involved in a rat race and has become so engaged in their work and personal life. For such people, advertising is a great time- saver as advertising provides all the necessary information like product features, price, closest selling point, offers available and the like.

V. Society and Advertising:

Advertising is both a business and social force and institution. As a business and social process, it affects every-one in the society. The society stands to benefit as under:

1. **It uplifts the standard of living:** Advertising nourishes the consumer power and creates wants for better standard of living. Standard of living depends on the national income and its distribution on one hand and the consumption and saving pattern on the other hand with relevance to personal disposable income. Advertising gives potency to the consumption pattern boosting the total sales; which results in more, better, and cheaper production; increased production means more employment and

more personal income and, therefore, more spending. This ultimately improves the standard of living of the people.

2. **It generates gainful employment opportunities:** Advertising can generate more employment opportunities directly and indirectly for those who have expertise and confidence. Direct employment opportunities are wide open in the different branches of advertising. It is highly specialized and challenging field which requires the services of talented people like artists, painters, photographers, copy writers, musicians, carpenters, press men, actors and actresses, agents, and executives too. These people handle the different tasks associated with advertising.

   Indirectly, it has given employment by supporting all those industries that supply input to these advertising activities such as paper, paints, colors and dyes, electronics, steel and other metal industries. This employment generation is of notable importance to the developing countries like India.

3. **It provides new horizons of knowledge:** Advertising is a great educator. It is a form of education where every advertiser has something to share with the society. Thus, employer speaks of job vacancies and an idle candidate applies for job; parents hunt brides and grooms; producers speak of their products, service or the idea that they propose to sell. Each ad is a piece of information and has a theme behind. To convey the theme, the advertising copy tells a story, gives a statistical profile, gives enchanting illustrations that we have never heard and seen.

4. **It up-holds the culture of a nation:** Culture is man-made environment in which he lives along with others. It stands for the values of life and living. These values are subject to change and are guided by the dynamics of social, political, economic, and ethical dimensions. The cultural function of advertising is to understand, accept and represent the value structure of society before it vanishes.

CRITICISMS OF ADVERTISING

1. **Higher prices:** Advertisements today involve immense expenditure thereby increasing the cost of distribution. Thus, to recover the cost they charge higher prices from the customers.

2. **Materialistic living:** Advertising intensifies the need of people and encourages wasteful consumption. It persuades people to buy products or service which they do not need or cannot afford by making fantastical claims. People are even encouraged to buy products that are harmful for their health like liquor, cigarettes etc.

3. **Misleading:** Advertisers, sometimes, deliberately create deceptive advertisements to

misguide the customers by making exaggerated and false claims. Fake testimonials and fraudulent means are used to sell goods.

4. **Wastage of national resources:** Role of industries in Indian economy is unparalleled. Manufacturers create induced and exaggerated differences in the products to develop brand loyalty through advertising. The natural resources, capital and labor that go into production amount to wastes as these could be better employed in the setting up of new industries.

5. **Unethical:** Many advertisements are highly undesirable because they undermine values and ethics. Vulgar advertisements like that of Wildstone or Axe disgruntles public decency and encourages materialism in the society.

CLASSIFICATION OF ADVERTISING

1. PRODUCT ADVERTISING

Product advertising refers to the advertising and promotion of a particular product to attract customers and boost sales. It is the art of creating and retaining awareness of a product offered by the brand, rather than of the brand itself.

Objectives:

- To create demand for a particular product
- To make existing and potential customers aware about the product
- To spark off an interest about that product in the minds of the target audience

It is of 3 types:

(a) **Informative product advertising:** It seeks to develop an initial demand for a product. This form of advertising tends to characterize the promotion of any new type of product, for its objective is to simply announce its availability. Information advertising is used in early stages of product life cycle.

Example: An informative advertisement for a new automobile may stress safety features, a powertrain warranty and city as well as highway gas mileage as the primary product assets to attract consumers. A competitor launching a similar product may choose to advertise a different list of features that are typically optional or extra in other vehicles, such as a rear seat DVD player, heated seats and an inbuilt driving behavior tracking device.

(b) **Persuasive product advertising:** To develop demand for a particular product is the goal of persuasive product advertising. It is a competitive type of promotion that is used during the growth period and to some extent as well as in the maturity period of product life cycle.

Advertisers favorably use food to persuade consumers to buy. **For instance**, fast food commercials that show close-up pictures of a large, juicy burger, golden-colored French fries and a bubbly soda lure fast-food lover everywhere. A restaurant advertisement that shows couples or families enjoying the restaurant's food appeals to those who want to spend enjoyable time together. For consumers looking to lose weight, the convenience of pre-packaged, low-calorie meals induces them to buy.

(c) **Reminder oriented product advertising:** The goal of this type of advertising is to reinforce previous promotional activity by keeping the brand name in front of the public. It is used in the maturity period as well throughout the declining phase of the product life cycle.

Example: An advertisement of FedEx reminding customers about the discounts they can avail.

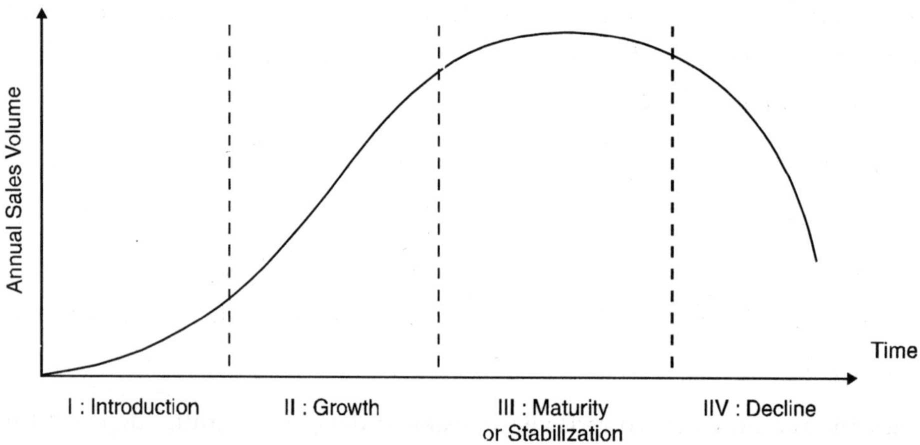

2. INSTITUTIONAL ADVERTISING

Institutional Advertising (also known as corporate advertising) aims to promote the image of a business rather than of a single product or service. The business also tries to promote its mission, vision, its philosophies and principles. Institutional advertising is also an effective way to create and sustain goodwill about the organization in the market. Organizations use this kind of advertising to promote good qualities such as reliability, low prices or good customer care, that distinguish it from its competitors.

Institutional advertising may be informative, persuasive or reminder oriented.

Example:

- Adidas, one of the world's leading sports brands started a campaign to donate 10% of their sales proceeds to the poor orphans of Africa. This was a typical example of Institutional advertising.

- ITC, a multi-business conglomerate, tied hands with CRY to promote their classmate stationary and donated Rupee 1 for every stationary sold. The stationery had an environmental message inscribed on it. Though one of the ITC's prime businesses was Cigarettes, they managed to earn a positive public image for the company.
- Another successful institutional advertising example is by IDEA Cellular, an Indian mobile network operator. Their advertising campaign "What an Idea Sirjee, went viral in Indian market and it targeted the growing issue of Corruption in India by launching an online campaign to collect ideas from the public. This found an instant connection with the public while simultaneously establishing Idea as a brand that cared about constructing a corruption free India.

3. ON THE BASIS OF DEMAND

(a) **Primary demand advertising:** Primary demand advertising is any form of marketing that stimulates the demand and educates the consumer about a product class. It is most useful when a new type of product is introduced in the market as it informs the consumers about the existence and benefits of products Primary demand advertising may also be useful when a product is losing market share or has fallen out of favor.

Example: "Beef. It's What's for Dinner" campaign is paid for by the Cattlemen's Beef Board, a conglomerate of producers and distributors, who have agreed that invigorating primary demand for beef is more crucial than promoting the specific products of any one distributor.

"Cotton: the Fabric of Our Lives" campaign which has made consumers more aware of cotton, and of the positive attributes (natural and soft) of cotton

(b) **Selective demand advertising:** This type of advertising is for a particular brand and the advertiser tries to present brand benefits that cause customers to selectively choose its product over that offered by a competing brand. This type of advertising corresponds with the general purpose of business, which is to distinguish your company from competitors to get customers and earn profits over time.

Selective demand messages are relatively easy to identify than primary demand ads. Selective demand ads typically identify the brand through name mention verbally or in written copy, or show the brand's product clearly. They often involve comparative messages whereby the brand tries to distinguish itself from another competitor by pointing out its strengths. Identification of unique benefits is a common strategy to indicate why customers should prefer the advertiser's brand over other options available in market.

Example: If the popular requirement is natural weight loss, then a yoga training center could showcase all the well-being activities they have through streamlined advertising and by highlighting their healthy and holistic weight loss programs.

4. ON THE BASIS OF TARGET GROUP

(a) **Consumer advertising:** Consumer advertising is marketing that is aimed toward consumers when access to a product may require an intermediary. It may utilize print, social media, TV, radio, and other forms of media with the goal of informing a customer about a product or reminding them of a need for such a product. It is also called *end product advertising* as it is directed towards the consumer. Marketers of pharmaceuticals, cosmetics, beverages, cigarettes, alcoholic beverages, and the like are included in such advertising.

Example: Nivea's advertisement campaign about men and women deodorants.

(b) **Industrial advertising:** This is also called Business-to-Business Advertising. This is done by the industrial manufacturer or his distributor and is so designed that it increases the demand of industrial product or services manufactured by the manufacturer. It is directed towards the industrial customer.It is targeted to individuals, who buy or influence the purchase of industrial goods or services for their companies. Industrial goods are products that are either raw material or component parts for another product, or are used for manufacturing other products(machinery), or that are used to help a company conduct its business operations (eg office supplies, computers) business such as insurance, travel services, and health care are also included in this category.

Example: an advertisement of Havell's fire retardant PVC insulated cables ensuring extra safety, double protection, perfect wire, consistent quality at no extra cost is an example of industrial advertising as it aims at generating awareness about the cables to other businesses like hotels, education institutions and the like.

(c) **Trade advertising:** Advertising targeted to distribution channel members such as wholesalers, distributors, and retailers are regarded as trade advertising. The goal of trade advertising is to encourage channel members to stock, promote, and resell the manufacturers branded products to their customers. Different media are chosen by each manufacturer according to the product type, nature of distribution channel, and resources at his command. Hence, it is designed for those wholesalers and retailers who can promote and sell the product.

Example: Coca cola advertising in a trade magazine "Progressive Grocer" to promote coca cola to store managers.

(d) Non-profit advertising: It is a growing part of the total advertising picture. It generally aims at fund raising, persuasion to action and attracting clients.

Example: Mahindra's #SeedTheRise

A crowd funding campaign was initiated in 2015 to improve lives of the farmers in partnership with Flying Cursor Interactive. It got donations up to rupees 1 crore which was matched by Mahindra by rupees 1 crore to add up to rupees 2 crore. This money would be used up for farmer welfare through 4 different NGO's. This includes improving livelihood, educating farmer's daughters and helping with agricultural advancements. A fundraising appeal film featuring actor Nawazuddin Siddiqui, a farmer's son was the core of the campaign.

(e) Professional advertising : Advertising targeted to professionals such as doctors, lawyers, dentists, engineers, or professors to encourage them to use a producer's product in their business operations. It might also be used to encourage professionals to recommend or specify the use of a company's product to the end-users.Manufacturers of these products try to reach these professionals under well-devised programmes.

Example: Pharmaceutical industry where decision is made by the doctors while the end consumers are the patients. Firms must direct their advertising to these decision makers.

5. ON THE BASIS OF GEOGRAPHICAL SPREAD

(a) Global advertising : International advertising is perceived as a response to global marketing enabling the agency to channelize advertising from transnational corporations into transnational media. The same product brand that was once sold nationally can now be sold to the globally backed by the same advertising claims.

Example: Coca Cola has been using the same standardized advertising in all countries. Pepsi adopts the common theme to the national culture.

Apple's minimalistic and intuitive approach has resulted in product's global appeal. Apple site is carefully designed and localised for international audiences.

(b) National advertising : National advertising is done by large companies on a nationwide basis or in most regions of the country. Most of the advertisements of well-known companies and brands that are seen on television or internet or in other major national or regional media are examples of national advertising. The goals of national advertisers are to inform, remind and persuade consumers of the company or brand about its features, benefits, advantages, or uses and to create or reinforce its image so that consumers will be predisposed to purchase it.

Examples: BPL (Believe in the best). Whirlpool Refrigerator (Fast Forward Ice Simple) etc

(c) Regional advertising : If the manufacturer confines his advertising to a single region of the country, its promotional effort is called Regional Advertising. This can be done by the manufacturer, wholesaler, or retailer of the firm. Advertisements of newspapers covering those states or districts where these newspapers are circulated is known as regional advertising.

Example: The Assam Tribune (only for the NE region) etc.

(d) Local advertising : Advertising is done by retailers to local merchants to encourage consumers to shop at a specific store or use a local service or patronize a particular establishment. Retail or local advertising tends to emphasize specific patronage motives such as price, hours of operation, service, atmosphere, image, or merchandise assortment. Retailers are concerned with building store traffic, so that their promotions often take the form of direct-action advertising designed to produce immediate store traffic and sales.

Example: Advertisements of Ooo la la, Gupshup (Local FM channels) etc.

6. SERVICE ADVERTISING

Services are activities, benefits or satisfactions offered for sale and they are intangible, variable, and perishable. In recent years, service sector has expanded quite fast and major service industries like banks, airlines hotels advertise heavily. The main industries are:

- Hotel
- Service
- Transportation industries
- financial services

Example: SHARDA university: the world is here, where are you?

7. PUBLIC SERVICE ADVERTISING

It is a message in the public interest disseminated without charge, with the objective of raising awareness, changing public attitudes and behavior towards a social issue. Public service announcements can be used to generate awareness of an issue or a cause. For example, a stop smoking campaign, or a buckle-up seatbelt initiative often releases PSAs that have catchy, memorable one-line taglines or slogans are usually easy for people to remember. Unlike paid advertising, which allows a company to promote specific features of its product or service, PSAs are intended to generate awareness or issue calls to action rather than sell something *specific*. David Ogilvy who is one of the pioneers of advertising and marketing concepts had reportedly encouraged the use of advertising field for a social cause.

Example: an advertisement on traffic rules is PSA: "Obey traffic signs, or overtakes your fate"

8. PUBLIC RELATIONS ADVERTISING

It is a part of institutional advertising. The most widely accepted definition is "the deliberate and sustained effort to establish and maintain mutual understanding between an organization and public." It represents management's policies and performances to public. Public relations advertising re means 90 p.c. doing and 10 p.c. talking about it.

Example: GOOGLE's fight against EBOLA:

While governments were discussing the best approach towards EBOLA, GOOGLE stepped up and its CEO pledged $2 for every dollar donated through its website by a specific URL onetoday.google.com/fightebola.

9. ADVERTISING ACCORDING TO THE TIMING OF RESPONSE:

(a) **Direct action advertising:** Sometimes advertisements are designed to get the audience response immediately. These types of advertisements are called direct-action advertisements.

Example: an advertisement of "Hit: why let flies get nosy?" in summers induces customers to buy the product right away.

(b) **Indirect action advertising:** This type of advertising exercise is carried out to make a positive effect on the mind of the reader or viewer. After getting the advertisement he does not rush to buy the product, but he develops a favorable image of the brand in his mind.

Example: an advertisement of "Electrolux: India's only total wash technology, uses less detergents and less water" induces customers to buy the product but as it is of high value the customers evaluate their options in the market bringing out change in their attitude and finally the customer makes the purchase decision.

10. CONVERGENCE ADVERTISING

Multi-product highly diversified companies choose communication packages highlighting their core skills or strengths or mother technology. Here, the core skills are leveraged. The synergistic effect is emphasized. Sony has entered computers and resorted to convergence advertising transferring its halo from entertainment to PC's. Daewoo compares its mother technology to human brain, and other anatomical parts and their launches are equated with each other. Convergence advertising is used for complex technical products.

11. ADVERTISING ACCORDING TO MEDIUM UTILIZED

The broad classification based on media is as follows.

- **Audio advertising,** which is done through radio, P A systems, auto-rickshaw promotions, and four-wheeler promotions etc.
- **Visual advertising** which includes POP displays, without text catalogues, leaflets, cloth banners, brochures, electronic hoardings, simple hoardings, running hoardings etc.
- **Audio-visual,** which is done through cinema slides, movies, video clips, TV advertisements, cable TV advertisements etc.

- **Written advertising,** which is done through letters, fax messages, leaflets with text, brochures, articles and documents, space marketing features in newspapers etc.
- **Internet advertising** is used extensively to promote products and services of all genres. For example, Bharat Matrimony, www.teleshop.com, www.asianskyshop.com etc.
- **Verbal advertising** Verbal tools are used to advertise thoughts, products, and services during conferences, seminars, and group discussion sessions. Kinesics also plays an important role in this context.

CASE STUDY: GOOGLE RESHAPES THE ADVERTISING WORLD

Rarely has a company grown so fast and in so many ways as Google, the company whose mission is to organize the world's information and make it universally accessible and useful." It was ranked as the most powerful brand in 2007. While Google provides internet users with a much better way to find information online, almost all the company's revenue comes from selling advertisements associated with search keywords. In 2000, Google launched a keyword targeted advertising program called AdWords that uses short text only ads to maintain an uncluttered page design and to maximize page loading speed. These are identified as sponsored links that appear on top or far right corner of the search page. Advertisers pay only when an ad is clicked (called cost per click) which in turn takes the web surfer to advertiser's webpage. AdWords run a specialized auction to decide which ads to show based on:

- Advertiser's Cost per click bid
- advertiser's quality score

Google recognized the importance of advertising and utilized that opportunity and now, Google is ground zero in a battle among traditional media and tech industry leaders and start-ups alike for the hearts and minds of world's consumer.

IMPORTANT QUESTIONS

1. Distinguish between advertising and personal selling?
2. Advertising informs people about the features, price and availability of the product. Hence, it must be appreciated and welcomed by all of us. Discuss.
3. Discuss the role of advertising in terms of Benefits and Limitations.
4. Explain the different parameters for classifying the advertisements.
5. Discuss the concept of advertising. Also explain what comes and what does not in scope of advertising.

❍ ❍ ❍

Chapter 2

ADVERTISEMENT ORGANISATION AND MANAGEMENT

INTRODUCTION

Advertising management is an arranged administrative process intended to supervise and control the different promoting exercises associated with a program to speak with a company's target market and which is at last intended to impact the buyer's purchase choices. Advertising is only one component in an organization's limited time blend and in that capacity, must be coordinated with the general advertising correspondences program. Advertising is, in any case, the costliest of the limited time components and hence should be dealt with consideration and responsibility.

DEFINITION

Advertising management starts from the statistical surveying stage. Now, the information delivered by showcasing research is utilized to distinguish what sorts of advertising would be satisfactory for a particular item. Gone are the days when there was just print and TV promotion accessible to the manufacturers. Nowadays separated from print and TV, radio, and Internet are likewise accessible as promoting media. *Advertising management process helps in characterizing the framework of the media crusade and in choosing which sort of advertising would be utilized to position the product.*

ADVERTISING MANAGEMENT

Advertising management comprises of various institutions like the advertisers, facilitating institutions and control institutions which supports the advertisers to develop an advertising campaign.

1. ADVERTISER

In the field of advertisement, the advertiser has always been the core institution. The total expenditure on the advertisements by the advertiser in the country provides a basis for determining the size of the advertising industry. Advertisers may be distinguished based onthe market they serve;based on goods and services they produce and the type of media they use. Further advertisers are classified as consumer, industrial and retail advertisers based onthe markets they serve. Consumer advertisers are mainly involved in the manufacture of durable and non-durable goods and services in the consumer market with the help of television, radio, and consumer magazines. Industrial advertisers specifically pre-dominate manufacture and market products for industrial markets more often by employing trade magazines, journals, business papers, trade shows and exhibitions etc. The local store patronage is advertised by the retailers with the use of newspapers which help with extensive coverage of the market.

2. FACILITATING INSTITUTIONS

There are three types of institutions which are regarded as primary facilitating institutions of advertisement management. Such primary institutions are Advertising Agency, Research Supplies, and the media.

- **The Advertising Agency :** The agency is represented as a position between the advertiser and the media. Its major role is the purchase of media time and space. The agency has conversations with both advertisers as well as media people. The advertising agency tries to make creative decisions as well as media decisions. Research by SRI center identified six attributes of agency as most important. These are creativity, account executives, media, top management, marketing, and research. It was also further analyzed that creative talent and knowing the client's business were the necessary strengths of the advertising agency.
- **The Media :** Through the years advertisement coverage has been influenced by media developments. Though there are many sources of media still printing press has made significant contribution to advertising. The printing press made newspapers and magazines on which most of the advertisers rely as the most viable sources for generating awareness. In the earliest time the advertising agencies were the agents of newspapers. The power of the newspapers comes from the dominant role in

localadvertising, especially by retailers. Whereas the industrial advertisers mostly use trade journals and trade magazines. Nowadays, magazines, television and radio have become the major media supporters of the success of advertising.

- **Research Supplies :** Research is the collection of information that can be further utilized to form evidence for advertising. These facilitating institutions comprise of various companies who provide research services to the advertisers, advertising agencies and media. Consumer surveys, customer measurement, panel copy testing, methods of media effectiveness are a few surveys which are provided by the research supplies to the advertisers. Development in the media and in the field of advertising has grown parallel to each other, making a significant contribution in creating and implementing the advertising programs successfully.

3. CONTROL INSTITUTIONS

Control institutions like government and competitors try to control the influence of advertiser's decisions making activities on the market players. The government implements various rules and regulations regarding the advertiser's product and services and advertising affect. It tries to ensure that advertisement serves its purpose of public service. Government tries to maintain a balance between the creative ideas of the advertisers and its impact on society and nature. Another control institution is competition. Advertisers must be very careful while developing their advertising plan keeping in mind over the competition and for this purpose a practice called "**The Wall**" is implemented. Under this practice the editor and the publishers are restricted to interact with each other so that they do not influence each other while they are writing the advertisements. It will help to understand more deeply the competitor's strategies and content of advertisements can be improved while applying copy strategy.

The advertising activity for any organization may be handled in different ways. This creative task can be shouldered entirely by the advertiser himself or such responsibility can be passed on to the specialist house namely, advertising agency totally or it may be shared by the company and the advertising agency depending on the individual cases and circumstances. It is almost impossible to set a criterion as to say which is the best alternative.

ORGANIZATIONAL STRUCTURE OF ADVERTISING DEPARTMENT

The genuine determination is administered by essential variables like the measure of the association, the kind of the item, the nature and degree of market, nature of advertising work included and so forth. Be that as it may, the main role of any advertising organization is to give the methods by which the activity of advertising should be possible in the most effective, prudent, and orderly conduct. An internal organization shall be provided to the advertising department so that it can integrate advertising management functions with the overall organization's function efficiently.

Basically, the advertising department is the sub system of organization like all other departments. The association of advertising department, as an indispensable - some portion of organization association, is significantly and profoundly affected by the variables, for example, the status of promoting inside the organization, the number and kind of exercises framing the piece of advertising capacity and the degree to which the distinctive capacities and obligations of promoting are performed in the branch of advertising or done by the outside gatherings, for example, advertising agencies.

There can be five basic ways in which an advertising department can be organized. These are:

1. Organizations by functions

Organization of advertising department by functions involves sub-dividing the advertising works into sub-functional components. That is, the advertising manager would divide his total work into sub-functions like copy writing, production media and a person can oversee each function. This form is normally used by all those firms doing in-house advertising and performing large amount of their own production of advertising and sales-promotion work.

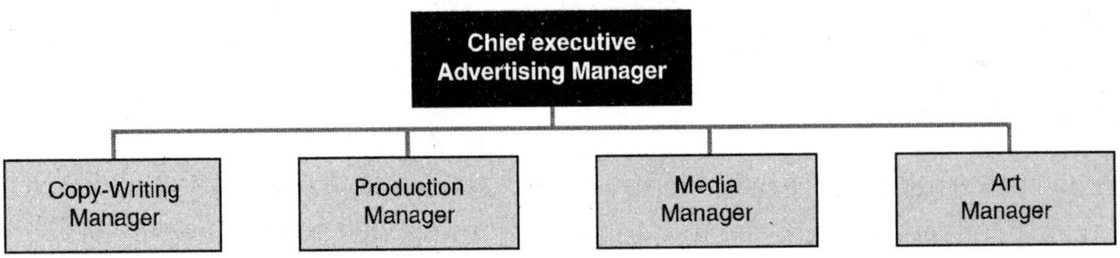

2. Organization by media

This type of organization involves the division of the advertising work by different media where skilled personnel specialized in each area or division of work will handle a task. These areas can be newspapers, magazines, radio and television, outdoor and mail advertising. Wherever such a type of internal organization is followed, usually there is a counter-part specialist within the advertising agency who works for the company to adapt its advertising to the particular medium warranted.

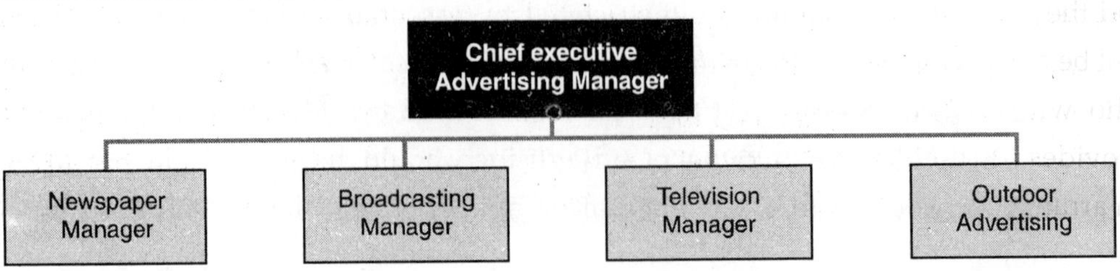

3. Organization by product

This type of internal organization is very popular with the large and diversified manufacturers, marketing consumer products or products. The basis for the divisionalisation is product. In such an arrangement, the manager is assigned the responsibility of the advertising functions for a particular product or a product group. Under such framework, the product manager is accountable for the coordination of advertising with crucial functions of each product area concerned.

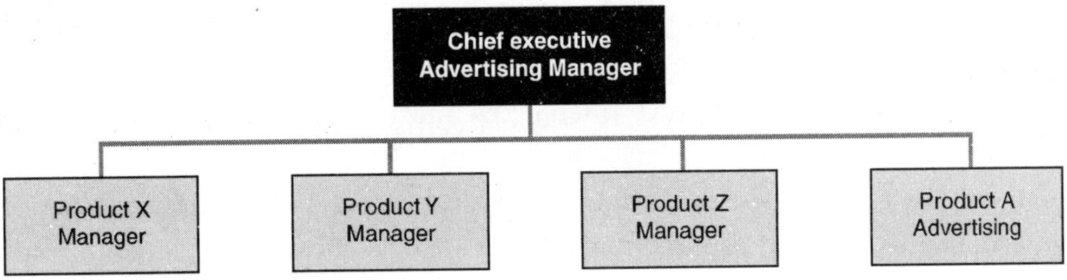

4. Organization by end user

The end user is the final consumer. Under such an organizational arrangement, the advertising manager is responsible for his performance in terms of markets or consumers. Under the direction and control of the ad manager, there will be area managers for each kind of market for the products.The rationale behind such an arrangement is obviously the fact that the same product story can be narrated to all the types of these products. It treats each market as a separate set of activities.

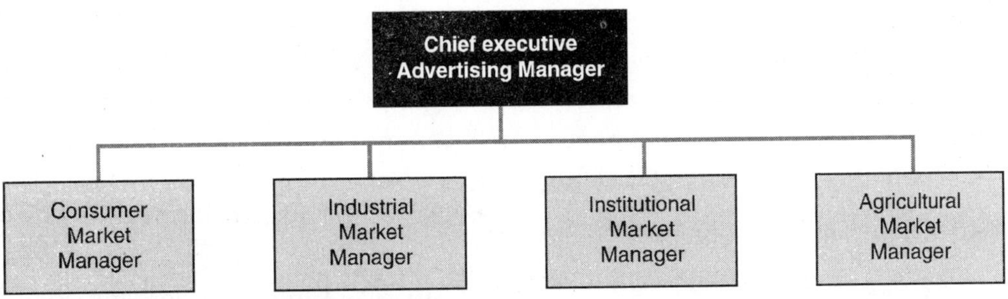

5. Organization by geography

In all those companies having wide-spread markets with individual geographical differences and the problems of customer taste and habits, such structure works well. Under the plan, there will be zones and segments and for each zone or segment, there will be an area or zonal manager who will further look after the advertising work of the organization.Such an internal plan provides for holding zonal manager responsible for total advertising activities. Normally, such an arrangement is parallel to the field sales organization.

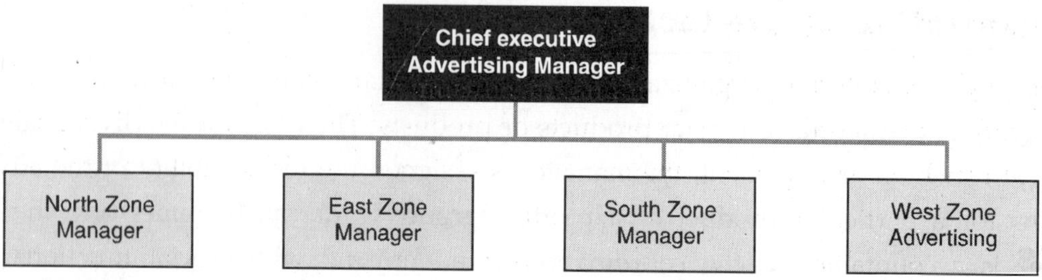

ADVERTISEMENT COPY

According to the UK advertising guru, David Ogilvy, 'people do read lengthy advertisements if they are skillfully written'. The most significant part of the copy is the headline, and sometimes even a small shift in the text brings magnanimous results. An advertising copy is a term used to describe the main text used in the advertisement. The text could be a dialogue, a catchy punch line or a company's dictum. It is a print, radio or TV advertising message that aims at developing and retaining the interest of the target customer and prompting him to purchase the product within a couple of seconds.

ESSENTIALS OF A GOOD ADVERTISEMENT COPY

An ad copy is made of various principles, all of which are integrated into a few lines of the copy that the advertisers are allowed to engage. It combines search engine optimization with marketing strategies and is used in all kinds of advertisements, not only pay per click and contextual ads. The essentials of a good ad copy are as follows:

- **Credibility-** An ad copy must focus on the credibility or the reliability of the ad. The copywriters should essentially flaunt an element of reliability in the ad so that the consumers are convinced to go ahead with the product. The credibility of an advertisement is the extent of honesty in the ad message. Misleading and misinterpreted ads harm the reputation of the selling house.
- **Attention-** The keywords, punch lines or phrases that seize the attention of the potential consumers or some component in the ad that attracts the target audience are essential in a good advertising copy.
- **Assurance of benefit–** An advertisement copy must contain some promise of the benefits that the product offers if the consumer purchases and uses the product.
- **Brief and clear-** An ad copy must be brief and clear, i.e., it must be to the point. It doesn't mean that the copy must omit the important elements of the ad. A clear copy is easy and quick to readfor the readers. It is self-explanatory, definite, and precise. Clarity makes way for interpretation.
- **Apt and conforming-** The copy must be apt and must match the needs of the prospects.

A copywriter must use the most suitable USP. Every ad copy must meet the conforming standards and rules acceptable to the advertising media and the laws of the land. A copy that offends morality challenges religious beliefs of the people is not welcomed by any media.

TYPES OF ADVERTISING COPY

Depending on various objectives for which advertising copy are prepared, advertising copy can be of following types:

- **Scientific Copy:** Scientific copy is of a technicalnature, and it provides details regarding the producer and the product. This type of copy is generally used by engineering and drug & pharmaceutical firms to inform ordinary people in general and professional persons in particular about the merits and value of the product so that they may be stimulated to buy it.
- **Descriptive Copy:** This copy is non-technical in nature and is prepared in such a manner that a layman can understand it. It gives detailed information about the product in very simple language. This type of advertisement copy is generally used for the products which are purchased as a matter of routine.
- **Topical Copy:** Topical copy is that advertisement copy which is intended to appeal the target prospects by establishing a connection between the product and a particular recent happening. This type of copy commands a good deal of interest because of that sensational event which are fresh in the minds of the prospects. For example – advertising copy of Adidas during sports.
- **Narrative Copy:** Under this type of copy, appeals are made to the prospects with the help of fictitious stories which narrate the benefits of purchasing the product. Generally, the story covered under this copy is humorous and carries the message in an appealing manner which can be remembered by the public easily.
- **Personality Copy**: This type of advertisement copy attempts to encash the opinion of an important personality about the product. Personality advertisement copies are quite popular now a day on television. For instance – Salman Khan in Revital.
- **Questioning Copy:** Questioning copy includes several questions expected to be answered by the prospects. The answer to these questions lies in the use of the product advertised. For example, advertisement of Godrej Locks.
- **Suggestive Copy:** Suggestive copies are those advertisement copies which try to suggest the audience directly or indirectly for pursuing them to purchase a particular product. It is particularly useful in those products where the prospects are confused about the

quality of different brands. For example, Advertisement done through Medifact about Complan.

- **Reason Why Copy**: In this type of advertising,a copy advertised message explains why it is necessary to have the product. It gives definite positive points in favour of a particular product. For example, advertisement copy used in insurance sector like LIC.
- **Fear Copy:** Those advertising copy which appeal to the sense of fear of prospects come under this category. These copies arouse deep interest in the prospect for protecting their valuables. For example, Advertisement of locks, medical and insurance sector etc.

STRUCTURE OF ADVERTISING COPY

Attainment of advertising objectives largely depends on the way the advertisement copy is designed. The advertising copy should be designed in such a way that it is able to attract the attention of prospective buyers.

The following are the basic elements of the advertising copy:

- **Headline:** The most important element of the advertising copy is its headline. If the headline fails to attract the prospects, the remaining part of the advertisement is wasted. Thus, the main purpose of the headline of every advertising copy is to attract attention and create curiosity in the prospects. For e.g. – Desh Ki Dhadkan (Hero Honda).
- **Sub-Heading:** After the headline the next is sub-headline. If the headline has rightly suggested the value of product, the job of sub-headline becomes quite easier. Sub-headlines help the reader to have more knowledge about the product. For e.g. – sub-headline used in Horlicks ad – Dudh Mein Horlicks Milao, Dudh Ki Shakti Badhao.
- **Slogans:** A slogan is the group of words regularly used by the advertiser to impress prospects about the product and producer. It is one of the most popular methods to attaining and holding the attention of the customers. For e.g. – McDonald – I'm loving it.
- **Text or Body:** After headline, sub-headline and slogan comes the text of advertising copy. In the text, both the rational and emotional reasons are put forward to persuade customers to buy the brand. Facts and figures about the product, guarantee of satisfactory performance, testimonials, etc. are given in the text of the advertisement copy depending upon the nature, competition, market, etc.
- **Closing Idea:** Finally, advertising copy should close the idea with enough information, direction and motivation for the customer to act. Various types of closing ideas are "buy now", "visit the nearest store today", etc.

CASE STUDY: WPP (J. WALTER THOMPSON AND OGILVY SOUTH ASIA)

WPP began life as a manufacturer of wire shopping baskets. Today it is the world leader in communications services. **J. Walter Thompson and Ogilvy** are subsidiary companies of WWP. **J. WALTER THOMPSON:** Its subsidiary J. Walter Thompson is South Asia leading market communication agency, it provides powerful 360-degree solutions to its clientele worldwide through its interconnected business in Mumbai, New Delhi, Kolkata, Chennai, Hyderabad and Bangalore. The group has three agencies out of which two are digital agencies and the other is a Rural Shopper and experimental company. These agencies are:

- **Hungama Digital Service** provides gamut of digital solutions across platforms and mediums. On offer are creative and promo marketing services, viral marketing campaigns, social media marketing and mobile marketing, applications, managing websites and video services.
- **Mirum** creates experiences that people want and businesses need. Named a Visionary in the 2016 Gartner Magic Quadrant, Mirum helps guide brands in business transformation, experience development, and commerce and activation. The agency operates in 20 countries, with more than 46 offices and 2,200 professionals.
- **Geometry Global Encompass Network** is a bustling hub of creativity. Powered by ardent, driven people who have mastered the art of working hard and partying even harder, this is where imagination really comes alive. Passion dictates everything they do and it's evident in the powerful brand strategies and engagements that we design and implement. Catering to an array of mega brands like Hyundai, Eicher, Google, Airtel, Pepsi, Audi, Asian Paints, Mercedes, P&G and BMW, they thrive on their zeal to constantly re-invent ideas.

OGILVY SOUTH ASIA: Ogilvy South Asia is the subsidiary of WPP founded by David Ogilvy in 1948. Today, there is one Ogilvy, in 83 countries and 132 offices. They consider themselves as one doorway to a creative network, re-founded to make brands matter in a complex, noisy, hyper-connected world. It has contributed to many ad campaigns like that of Fevicol, Fevikwik, Cadbury Dairy milk, Vodafone zoozoo, Anti-smoking and many more in the list. One of its campaigns under the former creative director Piyush Pandey was the most successful campaign. The movement was named**Bell Bajao- Bring domestic violence to a halt**. It encouraged the residents to take a step forward towards the physical abuse against women through simple acts of domestic violence. Boman Irani emphasized men to take a step against physical abuse against women. The campaign motivated people to stop the violence in their nearest places by ringing the bells of the houses.

Ogilvy South Asia also provided their expertise to the Tourism Ministry of India to create a new campaign to increase the number of tourists in India. The basic idea of the campaign was to highlight India's rich heritage and culture and history like yoga, spirituality, and Ayurveda. The campaign was conducted globally and it received positive remarks from the travelers. Indian personalities like Amitabh Bachchan, Aamir Khan, Priyanka Chopra were hired as brand ambassadors for the campaign.

IMPORTANT QUESTIONS

1. Explain the concept and scope of advertising management.
2. What are the major institutions in advertising management?
3. What are the components of advertising?
4. What are the various parameters for classification of advertising organizations?

❍ ❍ ❍

Chapter 3

ADVERTISEMENT PLANNING AND DECISION MAKING

INTRODUCTION

Advertising planning is a qualitative aspect. It adds value to the advertisements which are made. The main concern of the advertising people is planning the advertisement in such a way that it adds value to the product and meaning to the brand to which buyers can relate. Advertising planning is just like preparing a blueprint of tactic knowledge into black and white. The development of advertising plan is to identify various alternatives of expenditure, objectives and strategies and options with selection of media for finalizing the advertisements. Advertising planner needs creative strength to perform efficiently. Advertising requires fulfilling three main manifestations of brand i.e.

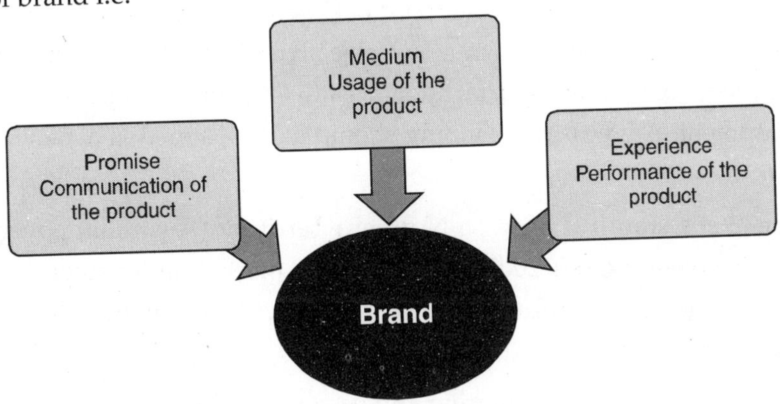

ADVERTISING PLANNING AND DECISION MAKING

Advertising planning is the foremost step to be undertaken before making an advertisement. Though the advertising planning process differs from company to company but generally the following steps are followed to develop a successful advertising planning process.

1. STUDY OF MACRO AND MICROENVIRONMENT

Macro and Microenvironment are two main aspects of the market which need to be analyzed by the advertiser before planning to make an advertisement. Macro environment is external in nature including economic, political, social, ethical, physical, and technological disciplines, whereas micro environmental factors comprise of factors which internally influence the organization like historical background of the organization, life philosophy, culture, strength, opportunities and threats. The extent of influence of the factors can be studied by analyzing market, industry, and company.

- **Market analysis** includes factors like relevant social, political, economic, and technological having effect on the nature and extent of demand of product, size of the market and stages of product life cycle.
- **Industry analysis** includes comparison of own industry share with other industries in the market and reviewing the influence of economic and political factors and market forces of demand and supply on the ways of development of an industry.
- **Company analysis** comprises of till-date growth of the company by measuring its past performance, profitability, future growth and prospects, finances, management structure and market share.

2. SETTING OF ORGANIZATIONAL GOALS

In the logical frameworks approach, the term "objectives" refers to the precise sub-goals to be attained to eventually fulfill the campaign goal. Reaching these objectives is typically presented as the direct result of a campaign. Objectives pave the way for reaching the destination. Every company has its own set of objectives, mission, or vision. These range from profit maximization, consumer satisfaction, wealth maximization, social development to economic development. Advertising planning should also be aimed at achieving the objective of the organization.

For example,"Let's stop it... now", a Northern Territory (Australia) government campaign against domestic violence (2001-2003), using social marketing strategies with the general population and producing a resource kit for service providers, pursued three sets of objectives, linked to different target groups:

- **Victims:** Increased level of reporting and use of services; ending a violent relationship

- **Offenders:** Increased self-referrals to services
- **Public:** Increased levels of bystander interventions in domestic violence situations

3. DEFINING TARGET MARKET

In the highly competitive scenario, advertisers must set their target market before planning to position their product or service in the market. They should keep in mind the strengths of the competitors regarding their product and service. Target markets can be selected on various bases like income of the people, age, gender, geographical area, education level, climate, and culture, frequency of use of product, interest, and demand of the product. Segment represents the group of behaviour of individuals to whom company wants to serve their product and service.

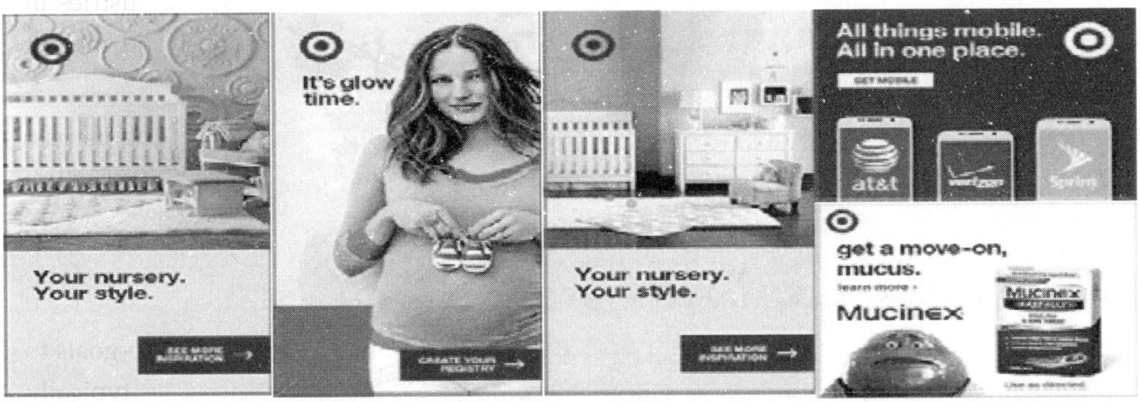

For example, a television show may be given a particular time slot because market research shows that people aged 13 to 18 watch television during that time and that is the target market the show is going for. Age is a demographic that becomes very specific to other factors: People aged 13 to 18 in the southern United States might listen to a different kind of music than those in the western states.

4. CONDUCTING MARKET RESEARCH

Advertising research is a specialized form of market research which aims to discover which ads will be most effective with the existing and potential customer base. These both are done through detailed research before a campaign and by analyzing the success of the campaign. The aim of advertising research is to understand your customers and their motivations better so that advertiser can produce better ads that demonstrate why their product meets buyer needs. Once the advertiser acquires an understanding of the people they are targeting, an analysis of the campaign will tell how successful the campaign was and help to iterate campaigns to continually improve results. To have an effective advertising plan, the advertiser should proceed with doing research about the existing market. Research here means finding out methods and analyzing facts to assist managers and to make rational decisions. Market research should focus specifically on the product, price, promotion, and place.

5. DEFINING MARKET OBJECTIVE

Marketing objectives are a brand's defined goals. They outline the intentions of the marketing team, specific numbers and provide clear actions to execute. Marketing goals and objectives are accompaniments to company's objectives and goals. The company's goals and objectives are revised according to the market goals. Generally marketing objectives involve growth, survival, productivity, profitability, innovation, creativity, increased sales, reduced cost, and quality of services. While designing the advertising plan, the advertiser must keep in mind the above objectives of the market.

6. DESIGNING A MARKET PLAN

Marketing planning like production, financial and advertising planning has its own relevance as it is one which links the firm and the markets. The market plan and advertising plan are documents of future course of action and help in appropriate display of firm resources to attain the goal.

7. DETERMINING THE MARKET STRATEGIES

Marketing objectives and goals are the basis for developing policies and strategies to decide the future course of action. Policies are the theoretical baseline which fixes the framework and tell the role of each individual whereas strategies show the practical aspect of the policies. They are the actions and counter plan to face market pressure. While designing of marketing and advertising planning a complete SWOT analysis of the market and competitors shall be done.

8. DETERMINING MARKETING GOALS

Objectives of advertising include reaching the maximum audiences, building a strong company image, improving relationship with dealers, increasing market share and profit share. The advertising objective is also to increase sales of its new products also. Therefore, before determining the goals the advertiser should identify the stage of development of a product in the market based onthe product life cycle.

9. PREPARATION OF ADVERTISING BUDGET

Advertising budget is a plan that determines the benchmark for advertising expenditure. The advertising budgets explain the classification of all the expenses and allocation of funds to the respective categories over a period. Advertising enables management to measure the actual performance to take corrective action.

10. TESTING THE ADVERTISING PLAN

Advertising planning is the most creative function of advertising. The planning of advertising should be done in an organized and logical manner. It should always be future oriented. Before showcasing the advertisement publicly it should be pre-tested among fewer audiences. Pre-testing will help in finding out the loopholes if any present in the advertising plan. Prior testing can help in determining the effectiveness of advertisement in future.

11. EXECUTING THE ADVERTISING PLAN

Execution of plan means implementing the plan and putting it into action. Now the main task is to see whether the plan works according to the set budget or not. Actual implementation of advertising plan will determine the effectiveness of advertising budget over a period of one year.

12. EVALUATING THE ADVERTISING PLAN

Evaluation of advertising plan means checking the actual performance and measuring it with standards set. This will help in finding out the real value of advertising plans. Advertising plans are assessed based on creative content and its effectiveness and whether the actual message has been imparted over to the targeted audience.

ADVERTISING STRATEGY AND ITS DIMENSIONS

An advertising strategy can be defined as a blueprint to help sell a given product to consumers. There are almost as many different advertising strategies as there are products to advertise, and each company follows its own unique strategy plans. The main ambition of every company's strategy is that their advertised message should be clear, precise, easily understandable, and noticeable by the targeted audience. The message should stand out from the competitors as well as in the market. An advertisement for cement should convey strength. An advertisement for moisturizer should convey softness and freshness. An advertisement for diapers needs to convey warmth and security. This way advertisement captures specific appeals to attract the targeted audience. Therefore, the advertisers try to focus on the main two dimensions of the advertising strategies.

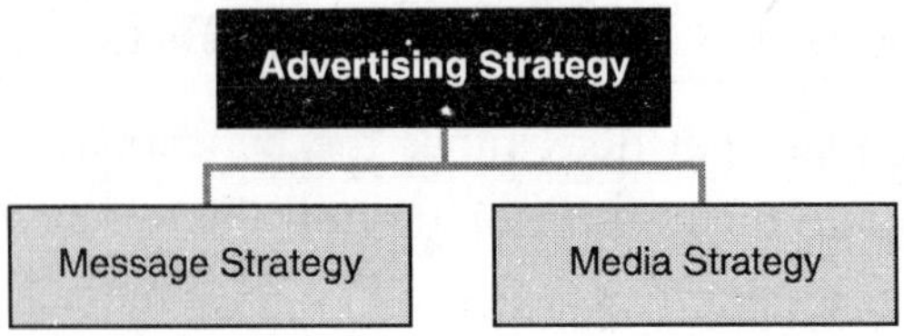

Any advertisement cannot reach all the people. It should have an appropriate mix of message strategy and media strategy with an unlimited budget. The two dimensions are elaborated below.

MESSAGE STRATEGY

Message strategy is an important part of advertising. The message strategy consists of objectives and methods. It determines the use of content in advertisement adopted to achieve the goals of advertisers.

Objectives of Message Strategy

1. **Brand Recall Objective :** The foremost objective of the advertisement is to make consumers remember their brand's name. The point is not only about remembering the name but to remember it at first instance whenever consumer recalls. Advertisers believe that the first remembered brand is high on popularity. Moreover, people relate to popularity, desirability, and superiority from the ease with which they remember the brand name.

2. **Link Key Attributes to the Brand Name :** Along with the brand name, advertisers want consumers to remember one or two attributes of the product. This type of advertising is closely related to 'Rosser Reeves' unique selling proposition style.

   Strategic Implication of the Unique Selling Proposition Method

   - **Resistant-** If an advertisement works and consumer can link that one attribute with the brand, it is unbelievably resistant to challenge that anyone can go to end remembering the brand.
   - **Big Carry Over-** The efficiency of advertisement depends upon the link created by it at first instance and is carried over by the consumer over the period.
   - **Expensive-** It will be expensive with lots of consumerlearning to the link an attribute that other brands are also trying to link.

3. **Persuade the Consumer :** The persuasion objective requires a significantly higher level of cognitive engagement with audience. The point is that in a persuasion ad, there is an assumed dialogue between the ad and the receiver. The receiver must think about what the advertiser is saying the receiver must engage in a form of mental argument with the commercial.

MEDIA STRATEGY

A message that is to be transmitted to an audience requires a media through which the desired message reaches its destination. This throws light on the importance of media in advertising. Advertising mediated communication needs the masses to reach out to the desired group of customers. In the process of transmission, the advertiser tries different kinds of media to win the masses.

In developing a media plan, three basic strategies are adopted:

1. **The National Plan Strategy :** This strategy is adopted by those advertisers who have a nationwide market for their products and therefore they advertise naturally to reach the people living in every corner of the nation. Such people are the target market for the advertiser.
2. **The Key Market Plan Strategy :** A media strategy based on division of the market into geographic segments may be called a key market approach. Key market strategy can also be employed by the advertisers who have national distribution for their products but the funds available for advertising are limited.
3. **The Skin Plan Strategy :** Under this plan, market segmentation is based upon specific factors such as income level, educational level, occupation, social status etc. Here the goal of the advertiser is to concentrate advertising upon those people who are most likely to be the buyer of his product. After the first segment is decided and sales is worked out the advertiser proceed towards the identification of new segment. The process of identification will continue till the product has been accepted by the mass market. If the product does not get universal acceptability, the advertiser will market the product in the limited segment market.

Thus, both message strategy and media strategy are equally important to have a well-planned advertising strategy. A well-structured and well-planned advertising strategy will help advertiser to create an image of brand in the mind of targeted audiences.

IMPORTANT QUESTIONS

1. What are different dimensions of advertising strategies? Explain in detail.
2. Explain different steps in advertising planning process.
3. What do you mean by advertising planning?
4. What is the role of media and message strategy analysis in advertising planning?

❍❍❍

Chapter 4

SEGMENTATION AND POSITIONING

INTRODUCTION

Rahul felt hungry while studying at night. Away from home, he wanted somebody to make something for him to eat as he did not want to go outside to get something to eat. It was 3 a.m. at night. He finally went out and found something to eat from roadside vendor. This incident made him aware of a business opportunity. After completing his education, he thought of venturing into food business with the concept of delivering food at night. As a student he always felt the need of midnight snack and found that many youngsters were facing same problem. He finally started a business named "Night Cravings" that intended to deliver food throughout night. In this way he segmented his food products for the students studying at night and have cravings for snacking while studying.

The process of segmenting your target market into smaller groups based on their shared traits, requirements, preferences, or behaviours is known as market segmentation. By dividing your market into several segments, you may provide each one a more pertinent and gratifying answer by customizing your marketing mix (product, price, place, and promotion). Market segmentation can be done using a number of different factors, including demographics, geography, psychographics, and behaviour. Once the markets are segmented, it is necessary to select the appropriate marketing mix for the identified segments. Be it product decisions. pricing decisions, place decisions or promotion mix, everything need special attention with reference to the market segment.Clearly, most brands today cannot afford to just be one image and one selling message to one huge homogenous market out there. It is more important than ever to target specific customer groups, with specific messages. The advertising decision maker must determine which consumer groups or market segments are most likely to respond favorably to the competitive advantages of the advertised brand based on this analysis. This identification of high-potential market groups is typically supported by the process of choosing precisely which part of the brand should dominate the advertising, as the competitive strengths of the brand can depend on how the brand is represented. What "position" must the brand occupy in consumers' minds in terms of the overall impression or picture that is left behind?

SEGMENTATION STRATEGY

A company's strategy for identifying each sector of its target market is referred to as a segmentation strategy in marketing terms. Businesses create a segmentation plan to correctly classify their clients and select the best markets for their goods and advertising. A segmentation strategy can be as simple as a list of your target consumers or as detailed as a manual for making short- and long-term strategies to interact with various audiences.

Almost any criterion, such as demographics, consumer behaviour, location, lifestyle, and personality, can be used to define a market segment. A successful segmentation approach can concentrate on several distinct segments or segments that overlap and take diverse combinations of variables into account. One company's segmentation strategy, for instance, would be to target customers according to where they reside. A different corporation might develop market categories based on the intersection of age and lifestyle preferences.

Market segmentation strategy involves the development and pursuit of marketing programs directed at subgroups of the population that an organization or firm could potentially serve. A variety of marketing tools can be utilized to implement a segmentation strategy. Products and services can be developed and positioned for particular segments of the population. Distribution channels can be selected to reach certain groups. A pricing strategy can be designed to attract particular types of buyers. An advertising program can be created to appeal to certain types of consumers. Although the emphasis in this book is on the advertising plan, a segmentation strategy is not limited to any one element of the marketing program.

CONCENTRATION Vs. DIFFERENTIATION STRATEGY

Segmentation tactics come in two varieties. The first is the concentration approach, in which the company concentrates on just one subgroup and creates a marketing campaign for it. The second is the differentiation strategy, in which marketing plans are created for two or more distinct population subgroups. Undifferentiation, or aggregation, is the word used to describe the marketing approach that results when segmentation is not used, and a single marketing campaign is created and deployed to all groups.

Differentiated Marketing

Differentiated marketing occurs when a company creates campaigns that appeal to two or more different target audiences, demographics, or marketing segments. By targeting multiple well-defined customer profiles, a brand can build its customer base, master its niche, and begin to organically build brand awareness. For instance, a health supplement brand may use different marketing strategies to reach seniors, women or children with different vitamin products for each group. It might run TV commercials for older customers and loyalty rewards through social media for parents and younger adults. Proctor &Gamble , a leader in laundry detergents has various brands such as Tide, Bold, Drift, Cheer, Gain, Ivory Snow & Ariel. Multiple segmentation lets a firm diversify and minimise risks because all emphasis is not placed on one segment. Indian auto makers like Maruti-Suzuki and others are also pursuing multi-brand strategy.

Concentrated Marketing Strategy

A concentrated marketing strategy is targeted to one specific market segment or audience. For example, a company might market a product specifically for teenage girls, or a retailer might market his business to residents in a specific town. Concentrated marketing strategies are often geared for smaller groups of people, because they are designed to appeal to a specific segment.

Concentrated marketing can let a firm maximise per unit profits, but not total profits, since only one segment is sought. A firm with low resources may vie effectively for specialised markets. Shree Leathers, Shoemaker in Kolkata targets middle class customers segment for all of its shoes.

Differentiated Marketing Vs. Concentrated Marketing

Strategic Factors	Differentiated Marketing	Concentrated Marketing
Target Market	Two or more consumer groups are targeted in this approach.	One well defined group of consumers are focused under this approach
Product	Distinct brands or versions for each consumer group.	One bran tailored to one consumer group only.
Distribution	All suitable outlets- differs by each segment	All outlets are similar.
Promotion	All suitable media differs by segment.	No difference, same message through all medias
Price	Distinct price range for each consumer group	One price range tailored to the consumer group.

Developing a Segmentation Strategy

A segmentation strategy is a marketing concept that refers to a company's plan for identifying each section of its target market. Businesses develop a segmentation strategy to appropriately categorize their customers and choose the best niches for their products and advertising. A segmentation strategy can be a simple description of your target segments or an in-depth guide to short-term and long-term plans for engaging with different audiences. A good segmentation strategy can focus on multiple, specific segments or overlapping segments that consider different combinations of variables. For example, one company's segmentation strategy could be to target their customers based on where they live. Another company might create business segments based on cross segments of age and lifestyle interests.

Marketing professionals need to be able to create a customized market segmentation strategy to capture as many customers as possible using targeted product messaging. Following points to be kept in mind while developing a segmentation strategy:

- **Market Research:** Gather data on your target audience, industry, and competitors.
- **Identify Your Target Audience:** Define your ideal customers.
- **Segmentation Variables:** Choose criteria (e.g., demographics, psychographics, behaviour) for segmentation.
- **Segmentation Methodology:** Decide on the approach (e.g., geographic, demographic, psychographic).
- **Create Segments:** Group your target audience into distinct segments.
- **Segment Profiles:** Develop detailed profiles for each segment.
- **Evaluate Market Attractiveness:** Assess segment size, growth, and profit potential.
- **Select Target Segments:** Choose segments aligning with your goals and resources.
- **Positioning Strategy:** Determine how to differentiate your offering for each segment.
- **Develop Marketing Mix:** Customize product, price, promotion, and distribution for each segment.
- **Implement and Test:** Execute your strategy and monitor its effectiveness.
- **Review and Iterate:** Continuously adapt your segmentation strategy based on market changes and feedback.

METHODS OF MARKET SEGMENTATION

1. DEMOGRAPHIC SEGMENTATION

Demographic segmentation assumes that people with common characteristics will have similar lifestyle patterns, tastes, and interests that will influence their purchasing habits. Demographics are often combined with other segmentation approaches to develop target markets with the greatest likelihood of buying their products. Demographics include factors like age, gender, occupation, income, and education.

(a) Age

Age is a valuable factor in marketing segmentation as it provides insights into consumer behaviours, preferences, and needs that often correspond with different life stages and generational cohorts. Understanding the life stages associated with various age groups is crucial, as these stages come with distinct needs and priorities. For example, a teenager's preferences and requirements are typically quite different from those of a retiree. Furthermore, age is closely tied to generational cohorts, such as Baby Boomers, Generation X, Millennials, and Generation Z, each of which tends to exhibit unique values, attitudes, and behaviors. This allows marketers to tailor their messaging and product offerings to resonate with the specific traits of each generation. Age-based segmentation is also essential for product development, as it guides the creation of age-specific products or product features that cater to the distinct needs of different age groups. In terms of marketing strategies, it enables the customization of messaging and advertising to directly address the concerns and aspirations of particular age groups. Marketers can also choose the most effective advertising channels by understanding the media consumption habits of different age groups. Additionally, age can influence price sensitivity, with younger consumers often being more price-conscious, while older consumers may prioritize quality and be willing to pay more. Age-based pricing strategies can be employed accordingly. Finally, age-based segmentation facilitates the creation of age-specific content, positioning products, and services, and tailoring marketing efforts to ensure they are relevant and appealing to consumers of different age groups.

(b) Gender

Numerous studies have suggested that there are significant differences in how men and women process information from advertisements. While it's essential to acknowledge that these findings are generalized and that individual responses vary, certain trends emerge. For instance, research indicates that women tend to engage with ads on a more detailed level compared to men, possibly owing to their heightened sensitivity to external cues. A female manager at Nike has found that women are more observing consumers and prefer ads that depict them as powerful and capable individuals. An empathetic Nike campaign has been successful in challenging gender stereotypes and empowering women. As baby boomers grow, it's important to understand prospective target segments, such as the aging boomers who respond to conservative values and home-oriented behaviours, and the under-thirty-five post-boomer Generation V consumers who are sceptical of hype and require more fact-filled, value-themed advertising. Different age groups require different advertising approaches, with teenagers and young children needing different approaches due to their unique processing of information.

(c) Income

Income is another demographic variable affecting segmentation. Unsurprisingly, households with greater incomes tend to be less price sensitive and place a larger importance on investing in higher-quality goods. Due to the rise in dual-income households, the share of overall economic spending that comes from these households has grown dramatically, which suggests that the market for high-end goods and services should grow significantly. The percentage of married couples with two incomes increased from only 29% in 1960 to 52% in 1990 and is predicted to reach 57% by the year 2000. According to one prediction, between 1990 and 2000, the proportion of homes with adults between the ages of 35 and 50 earning more than S50,000 will treble.

II. GEOGRAPHICAL SEGMENTATION

Geographic location can often provide the basis for an effective a priori segmentation strategy. Geographic segmentation allows marketers to group people based on where they live, work, or travel. The location has a significant influence on buying habits that marketers can use to develop their marketing messages. Even a little business can be dominant. if it selects a constrained region of land. Within the small area, it may be widely dispersed. You can use regional editions of important national periodicals as well as local media like newspapers or spot television. The local or regional business that limits its geographic scope and tries to cater its marketing approach to the needs of the local populace is the archetypal example of a concentration strategy. For example, McDonald's uses geographical segmentation to tailor its menu offerings to local tastes and preferences. For example, in India, McDonald's offers a vegetarian menu to appeal to local dietary preferences. Cadbury uses geographical segmentation to tailor its advertising campaigns to local cultural and social norms. For example, in India during festive season their advertising includes Diwali celebration, rakhi celebration and the like. The purpose is to connect with consumers during this important festive period.

III. BEHAVIOURAL SEGMENTATION

Behavioural segmentation is a pivotal strategy in marketing that involves categorizing customers into distinct groups based on the common behaviours they exhibit when they interact with your brand. Unlike other segmentation methods that rely on demographic or psychographic traits, behavioural segmentation focuses on how individuals actually respond to your products, services, and marketing efforts. This approach recognizes that customers' actions often speak louder than their stated preferences or characteristics. Marketers use a wide range of behavioural criteria to create these segments. Few of them are explained as under:

(a) Usage

Product-class usage, as an a priori segmentation variable, offers a natural and potent way to categorize customers based on their consumption patterns of a particular product or service. In many industries, it's observed that a relatively small group of heavy users, typically comprising about 20 to 30 percent of the total user base, is responsible for a disproportionately large portion of the total volume consumed. This phenomenon is commonly referred to as the "80:20" rule, where these heavy users contribute approximately 70 to 80 percent of the total consumption. For brands, having a substantial share of their user base within this heavy-user category is highly advantageous, as it often results in a significantly larger portion of units sold.

One effective segmentation scheme involves classifying users into heavy users, light users, and nonusers based on their consumption patterns. This approach is particularly valuable when the primary goal is market expansion. Each individual is assigned to a segment based on their level of product usage, and tailored marketing programs are devised to encourage increased consumption within each segment. These segments, defined by usage levels, typically necessitate quite distinct marketing strategies. While designing and implementing multiple marketing programs can be more resource-intensive than a one-size-fits-all approach, the potential market response justifies the investment. By targeting each segment according to their usage behaviour, companies stand to gain more significant responses and enhance their market share, making the effort and resources invested in customized marketing strategies highly worthwhile.

(b) Brand Loyalty

Brand loyalty can be a powerful basis for behavioural segmentation in marketing. Behavioural segmentation focuses on how customers behave and interact with a brand, and brand loyalty is a behavioural trait that reflects the extent to which customers consistently choose and favour one brand over others. Segments can include:

- **Loyal Customers:** Those who consistently prefer and purchase from a specific brand.
- **Occasional Customers**: Individuals who buy from the brand but less frequently.
- **Switchers:** Customers who often switch between brands.
- **Brand Advocates**: Loyal customers who actively promote the brand.
- **Churned Customers**: Former loyal customers who have stopped buying from the brand.
- **Purchase Frequency and Patterns**: Analysis of how often and how customers buy from the brand.

Using brand loyalty as a basis for behavioural segmentation enables marketers to tailor their strategies to these different customer segments. For loyal customers, loyalty programs, exclusive offers, and personalized incentives can help maintain and strengthen their allegiance. Occasional customers might benefit from promotions to encourage more frequent purchases, while switchers may need compelling reasons to switch back to the brand. Understanding and addressing the specific needs and behaviours of each segment can enhance customer retention, engagement, and overall marketing effectiveness.

For example, a retail company might use behavioural segmentation to identify and target high-frequency shoppers who are likely to respond to loyalty programs or promotions, while also identifying occasional shoppers who may require a different approach to re-engage with the brand. This data-driven approach not only helps in personalizing marketing messages and product recommendations but also aids in the allocation of resources more efficiently. Behavioural segmentation is an invaluable tool for businesses seeking to optimize their marketing strategies and better meet the unique needs and preferences of their diverse customer base.

(c) Attitude and Benefits

Attitudes, preferences, and many related psychological constructs such as motivations, perceptions, beliefs, product benefits, and so on, can also be used to segment markets through the second empirical segmentation approach. Customers can be divided into groups according to a variety of criteria, such as how they feel about your product (favourable, neutral, or unfavourable), what values they attach to it (environmental, social, ethical, or personal), what motivates them to buy it (functional, emotional, or social), what opinions they have about it (positive, negative, or mixed), what beliefs they have about it (rational, emotional, or cultural), or what preferences they have. Understanding client purchasing behaviour and communicating your value offer are made possible through attitude segmentation.Consumers differ in the "need" for which they buy the same product, so the fact that buyers will tend to place different degrees of importance on the benefits obtained from that type of product leads logically to the fact that they represent different segments. For example, in 1993, General Motors decided to segment the vehicle market not on the basis of physical size and shape (compact car, pickup, etc.) but rather on the basis of the need being satisfied (functional transportation, fun/ excitement, etc.)."

Segmentation strategy can be decided on the basis of specific benefits or solutions that customers seek from a product or service. For example, within the health and wellness industry, some consumers may seek weight loss as the primary benefit, while others may prioritize improved energy levels or stress reduction. Segmenting customers based on the benefits they seek allows businesses to offer more personalized product features and marketing messages.

In both cases, behavioural segmentation using attitudes and benefits sought enables companies to better address the diverse needs and preferences of their customer base. This, in turn, leads to more effective and targeted marketing efforts, increased customer satisfaction, and enhanced brand loyalty. Understanding the nuances of consumer attitudes and the benefits they desire is crucial in today's competitive marketplace, where personalization and relevance are key to success.

IV. PSYCHOGRAPHIC SEGMENTATION

Psychographic segmentation involves categorizing individuals into groups based on their personality, lifestyle, social standing, activities, hobbies, opinions, and attitudes. This approach works synergistically with demographics as it uncovers the underlying motivations driving people's decisions. Businesses employ psychographics for market segmentation to gain insights into:

- The way consumers perceive their offerings.
- The true desires and rationales behind consumers' choices.
- Identifying shortcomings or areas of dissatisfaction in their existing products or services.
- Recognizing opportunities for future interactions.
- Enhancing communication strategies for more effective engagement with their intended audience.

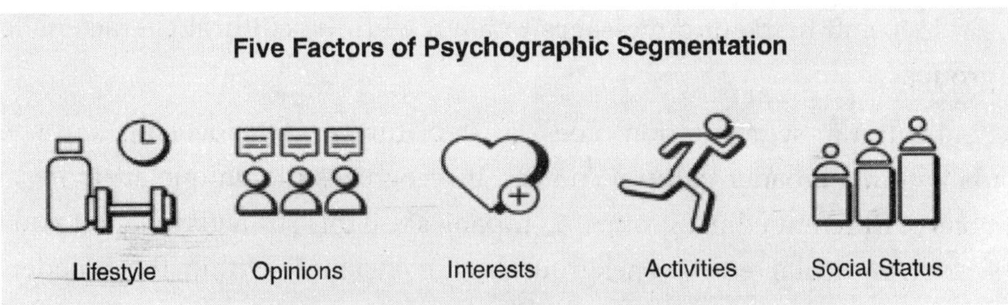

Example: Adidas, a prominent player in the highly competitive sportswear market, has effectively harnessed psychographic segmentation to stand out and create a unique connection with specific consumer segments. One illustrative example is their launch of pink sneakers.

These had been launched keeping in mind the fashion-forward girls who are highly influenced by peer trends of age ranging between 18 to 25. Adidas wished to position these sneakers as a fashionable staple in one's collection, catering to a consumer profile that embraces variety and trend-conscious choices.

In essence, psychographic segmentation goes beyond the surface-level characteristics of consumers and dives into the heart of what drives their decisions. It enables businesses to create products and marketing campaigns that align with the genuine desires and attitudes of their target audience, ultimately leading to more successful and meaningful interactions between the company and its customers.

V. CULTURE AND ETHNIC SUBCULTURE

Cultural and ethnic subcultural segmentation is a marketing strategy that divides a target market into groups based on cultural and ethnic backgrounds. This approach recognizes that consumers from different cultural and ethnic backgrounds often have distinct values, traditions, preferences, and behaviours.

Cultural segmentation involves categorizing consumers based on their shared cultural attributes. Culture encompasses a wide range of elements, including language, religion, traditions, customs, and cultural values. Businesses use cultural segmentation to tailor their products, services, and marketing messages to align with the cultural characteristics of specific consumer groups.

Ethnic subcultural segmentation goes a step further by focusing on specific ethnic backgrounds within a broader cultural context. It recognizes the unique attributes, experiences, and affiliations of different ethnic groups. Companies use this strategy to target and engage with consumers from particular ethnic backgrounds. For instance, within the broader category of Hispanic culture, businesses might create marketing campaigns specifically for Mexican, Cuban, or Puerto Rican communities, recognizing that each group has distinct cultural elements and preferences.

By employing cultural and ethnic subcultural segmentation, companies can effectively connect with diverse consumer groups, understanding and respecting their cultural identities. This approach allows for the development of products, services, and marketing strategies that are not only relevant but also resonate with the values and traditions of these segments. It also acknowledges the importance of inclusivity and diversity in marketing efforts, ultimately leading to increased consumer loyalty and brand recognition within these communities.

VI. FIRMOGRAPHIC SEGMENTATION

Firmographic segmentation is a B2B (business-to-business) marketing strategy that involves dividing a target market into distinct segments based on the characteristics of the businesses themselves. Unlike demographic segmentation, which focuses on individual consumers, firmographic segmentation considers the attributes of organizations. The key Firmographic Variables are:

- **Industry:** Firms are categorized based on the industry or sector they operate in, such as healthcare, technology, manufacturing, or finance.
- **Company Size:** Firms are grouped by their size, often based on metrics like the number of employees, annual revenue, or total assets.
- **Location:** The geographic location of the business, including factors like country, region, and urban or rural settings, can be a segmentation variable.
- **Ownership Structure:** The ownership type, whether it's a privately held company, publicly traded, family-owned, or government-owned, is a relevant characteristic.
- **Years in Business:** Firms can be segmented based on how long they have been in operation, from startups to well-established enterprises.
- **Number of Locations:** For companies with multiple locations, the count and distribution of these locations can be a significant variable.
- **Customer Base:** Firms can be divided based on their target customer base, whether they serve consumers, other businesses, or a combination of both.
- **Technology Adoption**: The level of technology adoption or digital maturity of a business can be a key factor, especially in tech-related industries.

This strategy helps companies tailor their marketing, sales, and product development efforts to meet the specific needs and attributes of different business clients. It's a valuable approach for effectively engaging with diverse B2B customers.

REACHING TARGET SEGMENTS

There are two ways by which markets can reach their targeted segments i.e. controlled coverage and customer self-selection.

1. **Controlled-coverage approach**: the objective is to reach desired target segments and to avoid reaching those who are not in the target segments. In this approach business carefully manages and controls its marketing efforts to ensure it reaches specific target segments or audiences effectively. It involves deliberate planning and execution to maximize the coverage and impact of marketing campaigns on the desired segments. Many companies are now creating immense computerized databases on their actual and potential customers. enabling them to execute extremely targeted direct marketing

programs. This technique is often called *database marketing*. For example,a high-end smartphone company uses the controlled coverage approach to effectively reach specific target segments. They identify two key segments: urban professionals and tech-savvy students. To reach urban professionals, they focus on business publications and LinkedIn during business hours, emphasizing productivity features. For tech-savvy students, digital ads on platforms like Instagram and YouTube are scheduled during evenings and weekends, highlighting gaming and entertainment capabilities. Budget allocation favours the professional segment due to higher potential value. Continuous monitoring and real-time adjustments ensure precision. Additionally, exclusive offerings, such as corporate discounts and limited-edition accessories, enhance engagement, creating a tailored and efficient marketing strategy for both segments.

2. **Customer self-selection:** Customer self-selection is an alternative approach. Here the advertising program is directed to a mass audience of which the target segment may be only a small part. Those in the target segment are attracted to the marketing effort since it is tailored to them. Those not in the target group will probably avoid exposure, not because the program is unavailable to them, but because they either consciously or unconsciously choose to avoid it. For example, a telecommunications company may offer a range of data plans with different data limits, allowing customers to select the plan that best suits their usage patterns and budget. This approach effectively reaches the target segments because it lets customers self-segment based on their specific needs, resulting in personalized services and higher customer satisfaction.

POSITIONING STRATEGIES

Just as segmentation involves the decision to aim at a certain group of customers but not others, positioning involves a decision to stress only certain aspects of a brand, and not others. A positioning strategy is a strategic marketing plan that helps determine where your business stands in the market and how it should be positioned to attract more customers. In marketing, a positioning strategy highlights the unique features that distinguish a brand from its competitors. It refers to how a brand wants to be thought of in the mind of customers relative to competing brands.

The set of associations a consumer has with a brand makes up the brand's position. These could relate to a person's appearance, way of life, intended use, persona, or even the retailers that sell it. A brand's position evolves through time through publicity, advertising, word-of-mouth, and usage experience. Depending on how consistently a company has advertised over time, this position may be crisp or diffuse. The perception of a brand in a consumer's mind is essentially a matter of comparison. It's about how the consumer assesses the similarities and differences between your brand and others in the same market. Consumer having a mental map represents the product category, and where your brand falls on this map concerning its competitors is what we mean by its position.

Approaches to Positioning Strategies

A positioning strategy is vital to provide focus to the development of an advertising campaign. The strategy can be conceived and implemented in a variety of ways that derive from the attributes, competition , specific applications, the types of consumers involved, or the characteristic product class. Each represents a different approach to developing a positioning strategy, even though all of them have the ultimate objective of either developing or reinforcing a particular image for the brand in the mind of the audience. Seven approaches to positioning strategy are as follows:

I. Using Product Characteristics or Customer Benefits

Positioning a brand based on product characteristics or consumer benefits is a common and effective strategy in the marketing world. This approach centers on highlighting specific qualities and advantages of a product, such as quality, durability, dependability, and style, which resonate with consumers. For instance, in the competitive toothpaste market, brands often emphasize characteristics that set them apart. Phrases like "refreshing" or "cavity-fighting" directly convey the benefits consumers can expect. Similarly, a slogan like "stronger than steel" emphasizes the strength and reliability of a product, making it stand out in a market filled with similar alternatives.

This type of positioning strategy is all about differentiating a brand based on tangible attributes that consumers can easily grasp. It aims to create a distinct image in the consumer's mind by highlighting the unique characteristics or benefits of the product. In doing so, companies seek to not only attract potential customers but also to build trust and loyalty among those who value these particular attributes. Ultimately, positioning based on product characteristics and consumer benefits can be a powerful tool in a brand's efforts to stand out in a competitive marketplace by communicating the quality and reliability of their offerings.

II. Positioning by Price and Quality

The positioning strategy that centers on the price-quality relationship and how consumers perceive the value of a product is a fundamental approach in marketing. This price-quality positioning strategy is instrumental in influencing consumer perceptions and purchase decisions. It allows companies to cater to various customer segments with differing preferences and budget constraints. This strategy acknowledges that consumers often equate higher prices with higher quality, and it leverages this perception to create distinct market positions. When comparing products, especially in segments like fashion, consumers may naturally assume that a more expensive jacket is of higher quality, leading them to associate it with prestige and performance. Conversely, lower-priced products are positioned as affordable alternatives, targeting a different segment of consumers who prioritize cost-effectiveness.

A classic example of this approach can be seen in the fashion industry. Designer jeans, often at a premium price point, emphasize their quality and exclusivity due to their higher cost, attracting consumers who seek luxury and prestige. On the other hand, department store jeans, more budget-friendly, target a broader audience by highlighting affordability and accessibility.

By effectively communicating the perceived value of their products, brands can carve out their own unique space in the market, whether that's as a high-end, quality-driven option or as an affordable, accessible choice.

III. Positioning by Use or Application

Another way to communicate an image is to associate the product with a *use,* or *application.* Knor Soup has positioned itself as an evening meal before dinner. Products can, of course, have multiple positioning strategies, although increasing the number involves obvious difficulties and risks. Often a positioning by use strategy represents a second or third position for the brand, a position that deliberately attempts to expand the brand's market. Thus, Gatorade, a summer beverage for athletes who need to replace body fluids, has attempted to develop a positioning strategy for the winter months. The concept is to use Gatorade when flu attacks and the doctor says to drink plenty of fluids. Similarly, Quaker Oats has attempted to position its product as a natural whole-grain ingredient for recipes in addition to its breakfast food niche.

IV. Positioning by Product User

Positioning a product through the association with a specific user or user group is a widely employed and effective marketing strategy. Positioning by product users, also known as user-based positioning, is a marketing strategy that focuses on associating a product with the individuals or groups who use it. This approach leverages the image, characteristics, or lifestyles of these users to create a compelling brand identity. This approach is rooted in the idea of crafting a brand's identity by linking it with the image, qualities, or lifestyle of a prominent individual or a particular category of consumers. By aligning a product with a well-known personality or a particular user group, companies aim to construct a distinct and appealing brand identity. Like in case of "Lakme" which has long associated itself with Bollywood celebrities to enhance its brand image. Actresses like Aishwarya Rai, Deepika Padukone, and Kareena Kapoor Khan have been brand ambassadors for Lakme which conveys a message of beauty, glamour, and style. An advertising campaign for a fitness brand may showcase real customers who have achieved remarkable results using their fitness equipment. These ads highlight the transformation of everyday people into fit and healthy individuals, emphasizing the positive impact of the brand's products on users' lives.

V. Positioning by Product Class

Positioning by product class is a marketing strategy where a product is defined and marketed based on its category or class within the broader market. Instead of emphasizing unique features or benefits, the product's identity is closely aligned with the general category it belongs to. This approach is often used when a product's features or qualities are like other products in the same class. The goal is to convey that the product is a reliable and typical representative of its category, ensuring it meets consumer expectations. This positioning strategy focuses on the product's essential attributes, such as quality, availability, and affordability, while downplaying distinctiveness.

An illustrative case is Dove, which has successfully set itself apart from the conventional soap category. Instead of positioning itself as just another soap, Dove rebranded as a "cleansing cream product" specifically designed for women with dry skin. This strategic shift allowed Dove to focus on its unique moisturizing properties and appeal to a niche audience with specific skincare needs.

VI. Positioning by Cultural Symbols

Positioning a brand based on a cultural symbol is a strategic approach aimed at leveraging a symbol of cultural significance to people and using it to create a unique and compelling brand identity. The key objective here is to identify a symbol that holds cultural importance and has not been widely utilized by competitors. By associating the brand with this symbol, companies can convey a distinct message that resonates with consumers. One notable example is the airline industry, where brands have successfully employed cultural symbols to evoke the concept of "royal treatment."

Amul's clever and witty advertising campaigns, featuring the Amul Girl commenting on current events and issues, resonate with consumers and evoke a sense of nostalgia. The use of this cultural symbol has allowed Amul to convey that its products are not just dairy items but also a part of everyday Indian life, symbolizing simplicity, taste, and a connection to tradition. This positioning has made Amul a household name and a beloved brand across generations in India.

VII. Positioning by Competitors

Positioning by competitors, also known as comparative positioning, is a strategic marketing approach that directly contrasts a brand with its competitors. Instead of focusing on the brand's own attributes, this strategy highlights the advantages and superior qualities it offers in comparison to rival brands. This approach can be particularly effective in markets with strong competition, as it helps differentiate the brand by showcasing its strengths in contrast to the weaknesses or shortcomings of competitors. For instance, a smartphone manufacturer might launch a marketing campaign that directly compares the camera quality, battery life, or performance of its product with those of a key competitor. By providing side-by-side comparisons or highlighting key features where their product excels, the brand can persuade consumers to choose their product over the competitor's.

It can influence consumers by effectively demonstrating that the brand offers superior value and performance when compared to alternatives. However, it should be executed carefully, as it may also provoke responses from competitors and lead to intensified market rivalry.

DETERMINING THE POSITIONING STRATEGY

Developing a robust positioning strategy is a fundamental component of any brand's journey to success. While this process may appear intricate and challenging, it becomes far more manageable when supported by methodical marketing research and a carefully decomposed, six-step approach. In this structured methodology, each step plays a crucial role in crafting a positioning strategy that not only differentiates your brand but also resonates with your target audience. These steps are as follows:

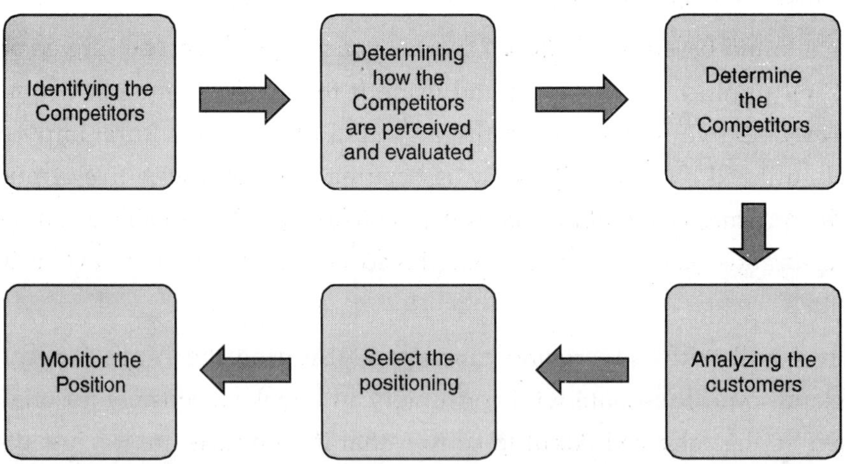

I. Identifying the Competitors

Identifying competitors is the foundational step in crafting a successful positioning strategy. It involves a thorough examination of businesses that operate in the same industry or address comparable customer needs. This comprehensive assessment of the competitive landscape is critical for understanding your brand's place within the market. In the mobile phone industry, brands like Samsung, Apple, Xiaomi, and OnePlus are competitors for brands like Oppo. While

Oppo competes directly with these brands in offering smartphones, it also faces competition from brands like Vivo and Realme. Understanding this broader landscape is essential for positioning Oppo effectively.

By expanding the competitive analysis to include not just direct competitors but also those addressing similar customer needs, one can gain a more comprehensive view of the market. This approach helps to identify potential threats and opportunities while positioning a brand strategically. It's not just about competing in immediate product category but understanding the broader context in which your brand operates, ensuring a more well-rounded and informed positioning strategy.

II. Determining How the Competitors Are Perceived and Evaluated

To determine how competitor products are perceived, it is necessary to choose an appropriate set of product attributes for the comparison. These attributes encompass not only tangible product characteristics and benefits but also intangible aspects such as product associations. It allows brands to emphasize what sets them apart while addressing the specific needs and perceptions of Indian consumers.

For Example: Smartphone Industry in India: In the highly competitive Indian smartphone market, brands like Xiaomi and Samsung often assess how their products are perceived compared to one another. To do this effectively, they consider a range of product attributes:

(a) **Product Characteristics**: This includes attributes such as screen size, camera quality, processor speed, battery life, and design aesthetics. For instance, Xiaomi might emphasize attributes like a high-resolution camera and a long-lasting battery for their smartphones, while Samsung may highlight their Super AMOLED displays.

(b) **Customer Benefits:** Brands also assess attributes related to the benefits offered to consumers. For instance, Samsung might position its smartphones as providing a premium user experience with enhanced customer support and services. In contrast, Xiaomi may focus on offering cost-effective devices with competitive features.

(c) **Product Associations**: Beyond tangible features and benefits, product associations play a significant role. For example, Samsung may associate its smartphones with innovation, quality, and a global brand reputation. Xiaomi, on the other hand, might associate its phones with affordability, value for money, and a tech-savvy image.

By carefully selecting and comparing these attributes, both Xiaomi and Samsung can gain insights into how their products are perceived by Indian consumers. This analysis helps them fine-tune their positioning strategies to highlight strengths and address weaknesses, ensuring their brands resonate effectively in the market.

III. Determining the Competitors' Positions

Another useful exercise is to determine how competitors (including our own entry) are positioned. The primary focus of interest is how they are positioned with respect to the relevant attributes. Analyzing your competitors' positioning strategies is a pivotal step in creating your distinctive market position. By delving into their marketing messages, branding, and advertising approaches, you can gain valuable insights into what values, benefits, or qualities they are emphasizing. This understanding of their positions can uncover opportunities for differentiation.

Consider a soft drink brand entering the Indian market, aiming to carve out a unique position amidst well-established competitors like Coca-Cola and Pepsi. To analyze their competitors' positioning strategies, they conduct the following:

(a) **Exploring Marketing Messages**: The new brand examines the marketing messages of Coca-Cola and Pepsi. They notice that both of these brands focus on youthfulness, happiness, and lifestyle in their advertisements. Coca-Cola's "Open Happiness" and Pepsi's "Pepsi Generation" campaigns are prime examples.

(b) **Branding and Advertising:** The new brand assesses the branding and advertising efforts of its competitors. They observe that Coca-Cola often associates itself with festive occasions and celebrations, while Pepsi positions itself as a bold and edgy choice for the younger generation.

By analyzing these aspects, the new soft drink brand recognizes that there is an opportunity for differentiation. They see that while Coca-Cola and Pepsi both emphasize happiness and youthfulness, there's a space in the market for a soft drink that positions itself as a healthier and more natural alternative. This could be achieved by emphasizing attributes like lower sugar content, natural flavors, or even eco-friendly packaging. In this way they can create a distinctive position that aligns with consumer preferences and presents an alternative to the existing market players.

IV. Analyzing the Customers

The next step is to identify your target consumers and what they want from your product or service. Understanding the target audience helps in pinpointing their unique needs, preferences, and pain points. This knowledge is vital for identifying areas where your brand can deliver distinct value. It allows you to tailor your positioning to resonate with your customers on a more profound level, addressing their specific requirements and positioning your brand as the solution to their challenges. In sum, a thorough audience analysis is the cornerstone of a well-informed positioning strategy, enabling you to stand out and connect meaningfully with your customers. This analysis delves into the intricate details of your customer base, aiming to understand their diverse characteristics, behaviors, and preferences. It typically involves segmentation based on demographics, psychographics, and behaviors.

Demographics entail categorizing customers by age, gender, income, education, and other quantifiable factors. For instance, in the fashion industry, a brand may discover that a significant portion of its customer base consists of young professionals with moderate income and a penchant for sustainable clothing.

Psychographics goes beyond demographics, delving into the psychological and emotional aspects of your audience. This could involve understanding their values, lifestyle choices, beliefs, and interests. For example, psychographic analysis might reveal that a significant segment of customers is eco-conscious and values sustainable and ethically produced products.

Behaviors focus on how customers interact with your brand. It encompasses their purchasing habits, brand loyalty, online behavior, and response to marketing efforts. By analyzing behavior, a brand might identify that a specific customer segment tends to make frequent online purchases and responds well to loyalty programs.

To conclude, a thorough audience analysis is the cornerstone of a well-informed positioning strategy, enabling you to stand out and connect meaningfully with your customers.

V. Making the Positioning Decision

The preceding four steps or exercises are essential precursors to the final positioning decision, as their outcomes typically wield significant influence. These exercises are versatile and can be performed subjectively by the managers involved if circumstances necessitate it. While marketing research is a more definitive approach, the process should persist even when research is neither feasible nor justifiable. However, even armed with this foundational information, one must bear in mind that there is no universal, one-size-fits-all solution to the complex question of positioning. However, some guidelines or checkpoints can be offered.

1. ***An economic analysis should guide the decision.*** The success of achieving any objective in marketing hinges on two fundamental factors: the size of the potential market and the likelihood of penetrating that market. For success to be likely, both these factors must be favourable. To assess market potential, it is essential to consider the current and near-future size of the target market. Demographic trends play a significant role in this assessment, and they can reveal growth opportunities. Other than this, the consumer lifestyle and attitudinal trends, helping marketers identify fast-growth areas. The "penetration probability" should indicate a competitive weakness to exploit or a competitive advantage to seize, ultimately leading to the desired market share increase.
2. ***Positioning usually implies a segmentation commitment*:** Positioning usually means that an overt decision is being made to ignore parts of the market and to concentrate

only on certain segments. Such an approach requires commitment and discipline, because it is not easy to turn your back on potential buyers. Yet the effect of generating a distinct, meaningful position is to focus on the target segments and not be constrained by the reaction of other segments. There is always the possibility of deciding to engage in a strategy of undifferentiation so that of attempting to reach all segments. Such an approach is risky and difficult to implement and usually would only be used by a large brand with a very strong market position. The implementation could involve projecting a range of advantages while avoiding being identified with any one. Alternatively, there could be a conscious effort to avoid being explicit about any particular feature.

3. ***If the advertising is working, stick with it:*** When a particular advertising strategy or message has proven to be effective in achieving its objectives, it's often wise to maintain that approach. Consistency in advertising helps build brand recognition, trust, and customer loyalty. Changing a successful campaign too frequently can confuse consumers and dilute the impact of the message. However, it's also essential to periodically assess and adapt advertising strategies to remain relevant and responsive to changing market dynamics, ensuring that what's working today continues to work in the future. In essence, it's about striking a balance between sticking with what's effective and evolving to stay competitive.

4. ***Don't try to be something you are not:*** While it might seem tempting to exploit a market need or opportunity, attempting to be something your product can lead to problems. It's typically naïve and detrimental to overpromise or misrepresent what your product can deliver. In the long run, customers are likely to be disappointed, trust can be eroded, and the brand's reputation can suffer. Effective positioning strategies should be authentic and truthful, focusing on the genuine strengths and benefits of the product. This honesty is not only ethical but also fosters stronger customer relationships and brand credibility.

5. ***Consider Symbols:*** Symbols play a pivotal role in shaping and communicating a brand's personality. These symbols encompass logos, icons, colours, and visual elements that become synonymous with a brand's identity. They are instrumental in conveying a brand's values, character, and positioning to consumers. A well-designed logo or visual symbol can instantly convey a brand's character, setting the tone for consumer perceptions. For instance, the golden arches of McDonald's or the swoosh of Nike are globally recognized symbols that evoke specific emotions and associations.

VI. Monitor the Position

Monitoring a brand's position in the market is a crucial aspect of brand management and marketing strategy. It involves regularly assessing and analyzing various factors to understand how a brand is perceived by consumers and how it competes in the marketplace. Conducting market research, Competitive Analysis, brand awareness, brand loyalty, and brand equity. These metrics help gauge the strength of the brand in the market.Gathering and analyzing feedback from customers, whether it's through customer service interactions, reviews, or social media comments is helpful in assessing the success or failure of a positioning strategy. Keeping an eye on market trends, shifts in consumer behavior, and emerging opportunities and adapting to changing market dynamics can help maintain a strong position.

Monitoring the brand's position is an ongoing process, and the insights gained from this activity help brands make informed decisions about maintaining, adjusting, or repositioning their identity and strategies to stay competitive and meet evolving consumer needs.

Case Study: How Is OYO Positioning Itself to Dominate the Market?

OYO Rooms, also known as OYO Hotels & Homes is the third-largest hospitality chain by room count providing a comfortable room stay and ensuring the acceptability of the services by the OYO's customers in more than 80 nations. Incorporated in 2013 by Ritesh Agarwal (one of the youngest Indian entrepreneurs, the founder, and CEO of OYO Rooms). It has established itself as the fastest-growing network of hotels offline and online. OYO uses a mix of demographic, geographic, and psychographic segmentation strategies to understand the changing needs of the customers in the competitive market. OYO segments the market in the following manner: -

- OYO Townhouse targets Millennial travelers
- OYO SilverKey caters to the needs of corporate travelers
- OYO Vacation Homes targets people who come on vacation at the beach or a villa on an exotic island
- OYO Life provides residential space

Targeting strategy is the cornerstone of the product development process. OYO uses a differentiated targeting strategy for different products categories.

- Corporate tie-ups for airline travelers
- Tours and travels
- College students or working professionals who are in search of fully managed homes on long-term rentals at an affordable price.

OYO uses a value-based positioning strategy for its customer by providing:-

- Standardized budget hotels
- Luxurious productive place
- Open grass greenery
- Better room service

IMPORTANT QUESTIONS

1. What is segmentation strategy? Differentiate between Concentrated and Differentiated strategy?
2. How a company can develop a segmentation strategy?
3. Explain in detail the different methos of market segmentation?
4. What are positioning strategies and explain the approaches to position a strategy?
5. How a company can decide about its positioning strategy?

❍ ❍ ❍

Chapter 5

INTEGRATED MARKETING COMMUNICATIONS

INTRODUCTION

For long, the promotional function in most companies has been dominated by mass media advertising. Companies rely on in house or external advertising agencies to guide them in developing a marketing communications strategy. Many marketers build a strong barrier around their marketing promotional functions and manage them as separate practices, with different budgets, different views of markets and different communications objectives. However, since 1980's, many companies began taking a broader perspective of marketing communication and seeing the need for more strategic integration of variety of promotional tools. This led to rapid developments in areas such as sales promotion, direct marketing and public relations which challenged the dominant role of advertising in marketing communications. This was a leap towards the integrated marketing communications.

INTEGRATED MARKETING COMMUNICATIONS

Integrated marketing communications (IMC) is a procedure which involves the management and organization of all 'agents' in the planning, implementation, analysis and control of all marketing communications messages, contacts, media, and promotional tools focused on selected target audiences in such a way as to derive the greatest enhancement and consistency of marketing communications effort in achieving predetermined product and corporate marketing communications objectives.

IMC can be defined as the management process of achieving greater brand consistency by integrating all marketing communications activities across relevant audience. IMC acts as a dialogue between the marketers and its customers and represents the voice of the organization and its brands.

Integration is challenging to achieve but when achieved, the 4Es and 4Cs of IMC create the harmonious benefits of integration.

The **4Es of integrated marketing communications** are:

- **Enhancing** – further improve the quality or value, intensify.
- **Economical** – giving good value for the time and money spent which is also, not wasteful.
- **Efficient** – maximum results with minimum wastage
- **Effective** – successfully producing the intended result.

The **4Cs of integrated marketing communications** are:

- **Coherence** – logical and orderly
- **Consistency** – not self-contradictory; in agreement, harmony.
- **Continuity** – connected and uninterrupted over time.
- **Complementary** communications – producing a balanced and supportive communication.

BENEFITS OF INTEGRATED MARKETING COMMUNICATIONS

Integrated marketing communications can create competitive advantage, boost sales and profits, while saving money, time, and stress even though it requires a lot of effort. IMC helps customers move through the various stages of the buying process while wrapping marketing communications around them. The organization nurtures its relationship with customers and consolidates its image.

1. CONSISTENT MESSAGES

The foundation of every marketing program is anorganized strategy and clear messaging instructions. After all, no one can tell where a customer may come across your brand. An agency that works with you to develop a marketing communication strategy for each channel as well as a story that you can be proud of will cut down the amount of time it takes for potential customers to recognize your brand.

2. GREATER MARKETING PRECISION

Getting potential customers to be aware of your brand is usually one of the first steps in most marketing campaigns. One cannot build a relationship with the customer until and unless brand awareness is created. Search marketing and pay-per-click (PPC) advertising are significant ways to raise awareness among consumers. These integrated marketing solutions highlight key messages and owned assets, making it easier for the organization to build rapport with consumers.

3. COST SAVINGS AND LESS DUPLICATION

IMC saves money as it reduces duplication in areas such as graphics and photography since they can be shared and used in, advertising, exhibitions, and sales literature. Agency fees is also substantially reduced by using a single full-service agency for all communications and even if there are several agencies, time is saved as meetings are conducted to harmonize work of different agencies. This includes briefings, creative sessions, strategic or tactical planning. This reduces stress as well as workload.

4. BETTER USE OF MEDIA

IMC ensures better and efficient use of different mediums available for creating brand awareness. The different mediums are integrated to represent "one voice" of the brand. This ensures brand recognition as well as brand recall among the target customers. This is the reason why most of the communications agencies design a well- planned communication strategy to get the attention of the customers. Carefully linked messages help the customers by giving timely reminders, updated information, and special offers which, when presented in a planned sequence, help them move easily through stages of consumer buying a product.

5. CREATIVE INTEGRITY

IMC recognizes the value of creativity that revolves around a variety of communications disciplines, for generating awareness among the target audience. This helps in fabricating strong, favourable and unique associations in the minds of the customers.

MARKETING COMMUNICATIONS MIX

The marketing communications mix consists of:

1. **Advertising** : Any paid form of non-personal communication and promotion of ideas, products or services by an identified sponsor via print media (newspapers and magazines), broadcast media (radio and television), network media (telephone, cable, satellite, wireless), electronic media (audiotape, videotape, webpage) and display media (billboards, skywriting, posters)

2. **Sales Promotion :** A variety of short-term incentives to encourage purchase of products including consumer promotions (samples, coupons, rebates, and contests), trade promotions (advertising and display allowances) and sales force promotions (contests for sales representatives)
3. **Events and Experiences :** Company sponsored activities to generate brand related interactions with customers including sports, arts, and entertainment activities.
4. **Public Relations and Publicity :** A variety of programs directed internally to employees or externally to customers, other firms, government, and media to promote a company's image and also, to create brand awareness.
5. **Direct Marketing :** Use of mail, telephone, fax, email, or internet to communicate directly with the customers and prospects is known as direct marketing.
6. **Interactive Marketing :** Online activities and programs designed to engage customers or prospects and directly or indirectly generate awareness, improve image, and boost sales.
7. **Word of Mouth Marketing :** People to people written, oral, or electronic communications that creates a favourable situation to buy the product.
8. **Personal Selling :** Face to face interaction between one or more prospective customers and the salesperson for the purchase of the products by making presentations and demonstrations.

PROCESS OF INTEGRATED MARKETING COMMUNICATIONS

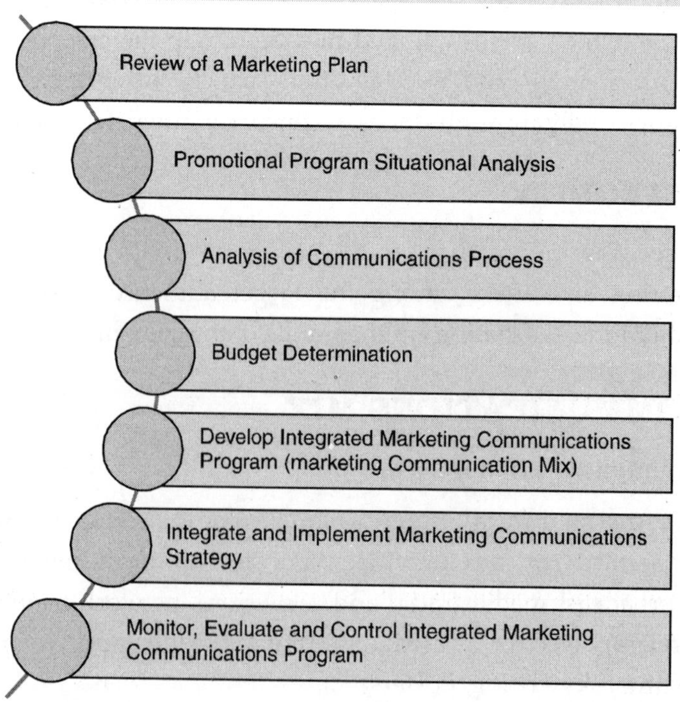

1. REVIEW OF A MARKETING PLAN

The marketers must comprehend where the organization has been, what its current position is and where it intends to reach and how. This information is contained in the marketing plan, which is a written document describing the overall marketing strategy of the organization. After it has been designed, the next task is to examine the objectives which provide direction to the plan and to assess the environmental influences by undertaking a competitive analysis.

For some firms, a promotional plan is a crucial part of marketing strategy and is developed like the marketing plan. However, it contains detailed information related to overall promotional strategy.

2. PROMOTIONAL PROGRAM SITUATIONAL ANALYSIS

After developing and reviewing a marketing plan, next step is to analyse the promotional program by conducting a situational analysis of the factors that are related to and affect the promotional strategy. This includes both internal as well as external analysis.

- **Internal analysis :** The internal analysis analyses the capabilities of the firm and the ability to develop and implement a successful promotional program. The successes and failures of previous programs are evaluated which stipulates whether the firm should opt in house agency or hire an external agency for the next program. If the organization had hired an ad agency for the previous programs, its performance is assessed which mainly focuses on the functions performed and the compensation charged by the agency. Another facet of internal analysis is that it appraises the brand image of the company i.e. how is the brand perceived by the target market. For example: Starbucks has an outstanding image that is a result of the quality of its coffee and its reputation as a socially responsible company.

  Also, the strengths and weaknesses of the product or services are gauged and acquainted to the creative personnel who design an advertising message for the brand. The focus is mainly on the unique selling proposition, price, design, packaging etc.

- **External analysis :** An important part of external analysis is consumer behaviour study which concentrates on consumer's perception, attitudes, lifestyles and purchase related decisions. Another key element of the external analysis is assessment of the various market segments to choose the target market and also, to determine how the product should be positioned. For this, a detailed analysis of direct as well as indirect competitors is done, which focuses on their specific strengths and weaknesses, their segmentation, targeting and positioning strategies, their promotional budget and media and message strategy. It also includes an analysis of the marketing environment and current trends that might affect the promotional program.

3. ANALYSIS OF COMMUNICATIONS PROCESS

This stage focuses on how an organization communicates with the customers in its target market and how consumers respond to such marketing communications.

• Communication objectives

First the communication goals and objectives which act as a guiding force for overall marketing communications strategy are established. This includes:

- **Category need**: Establishing a product or service category need is essential to remove any preconceived notions and to create a desired motivational state to purchase the product.
- **Brand Awareness**: Stimulating the customer's ability to recognize or recall the brand within a product class, is adequate detail to make a purchase by the customer. Thus, brand awareness creates foundation for brand equity.
- **Brand Attitude**: A brand's needs may be positively oriented (social approval, sensory gratification) or negatively oriented (problem removal, problem avoidance) and helping the customers to evaluate brand's perceived ability, establishes a favourable brand identity.
- **Brand Purchase Intention**: Driving the customers to purchase the product by giving promotional offers like discounts, samples and the like. However, if the customer does not have category need, it would be challenging to form buying intentions.

• Designing the communications strategy

Designing a communication strategy involves solving three problems:

- **Message strategy**: Different themes, appeals or ideas are searched in order to establish points of difference and points of parity of a product. This also helps in effective brand positioning.

- **Creative strategy**: Communication effectiveness depends on how a message is being expressed and what is its content. Creative strategies are a way through which marketers translate their messages into specific communications using an array of appeals.
- **Message source**: Messages delivered by renowned sources can effectively create brand recognition among the target audience, thereby increasing the sales. This can be done through celebrity endorsements, testimonials or brand advocates.

• Selecting the communications channel

Selecting an efficient means to carry the message becomes more challenging as channels of communication become more disintegrated and cluttered. Communication channels can be either personal or non-personal:

- **Personal form of communication**: this includes word of mouth, direct and interactive marketing, and personal selling.
- **Non personal communication**: this includes advertising, sales promotion, events and experiences, and public relations.

4. BUDGET DETERMINATION

After the communication objectives have been set, the next step is to determine the budget which incorporates focusing on two things:

- What will the promotional program cost?
- How will the money be allocated?

There are two approaches which can be used for allocating the budget:

Top-down approach	Build up approach
It is called top-down approach because the budgets are made by the senior executives and then the money is allocated to various departments.	In this, promotion objectives are set for the tasks to be performed. The cost of these tasks are ascertained and budgeted. The total promotion budget is then presented to and approved by top management.
The budgeting methods included in this approach are: – All you can afford method – Arbitrary allocation method – Percentage of sales method – Competitive parity method – Return on investment	The budgeting methods included in this approach are: – Objective and task method – Payout planning method – Quantitative models – Experimental models

However, the budget at this stage is usually tentative until proper promotional mix strategy has been designed.

5. DEVELOP INTEGRATED MARKETING COMMUNICATIONS PROGRAM (Marketing Communication Mix)

Companies must first allocate the marketing communications budget to different modes of communication – advertising, sales promotion, public relations, events and experiences, direct and interactive marketing, personal selling, and word of mouth marketing. Within a same industry the companies can differ in their choice of media and the use of budget allocation methods. Companies like Samsung, LG spend on Advertising whereas Eureka Forbes prefers Personal selling as a mode of communication.

EUREKA FORBES
Your friend for life

- **Advertising**: Advertising is a paid, non-personal form of communication which reaches geographically dispersed buyers. It can build up a long term brand image of the product.
- **Sales promotion**: Various tools like coupons, samples, discounts, contests, rebates and the like are used by companies to highlight their product among the competitors and boost their sales.
- **Public relations**: marketers overlook the importance of public relations, yet a well-planned PR program integrated with other marketing communications can be very effective to increase sales and market share.
- **Events and Experiences**: a well-chosen event can be highly effective as they are more engaging for customers.
- **Direct and Interactive marketing**: this involves communication through various forms like internet, phone, mail or in person.
- **Word of mouth marketing**: this can also take many forms like review by influential bloggers or brand advocates or customer's immediate reference groups like families, friends and the like, which helps to establish a positive brand image of the product.
- **Personal selling**: It is most effective in later stages of buying process and helps in building brand preference, conviction, and action.

6. INTEGRATE AND IMPLEMENT MARKETING COMMUNICATIONS STRATEGY

This involves integrating and implementing the promotional mix strategies of marketing communications. This evaluates a variety of communications discipline- and skilfully combines these disciplines to provide clarity, consistency, and maximum impact through impeccable integration of the communication message.

- **Integrating media :** Media integration occurs across and within different media types and marketers prefer personal and non-personal communication channels through multiple stage and multiple vehicle campaigns to achieve maximum reach and impact. Many companies nowadays, are combining their online and offline marketing communications strategies to enhance brand awareness. This eventually increases sales and expands the brand loyalty.
- **Implementing IMC :** Many promotion agencies, public relations firms, package design consultancies identify themselves as *Communication Companies* that assist the clients overall communication effectiveness by offering strategic advice for their communication strategy. Many international brands such as IBM (Ogilvy), Colgate (Young and Rubicam) and GE (BBDO), have opted to work through one full-service agency. The result is a much lower communication cost BUT more effective marketing communications.

7. MONITOR, EVALUATE AND CONTROL INTEGRATED MARKETING COMMUNICATIONS PROGRAM

The last step of this process is to evaluate the program's effectiveness and take measures to control and adjust promotional strategies. This is designed to provide managers with continual feedback concerning the effectiveness of the IMC program. For instance, problems with the advertising program may lie in message or media planning strategy that does not reach the target market effectively. The manager must know the reasons for the results to take the right steps to control the program.

BARRIERS TO INTEGRATED MARKETING COMMUNICATIONS

The concept of integration is considered inevitable by some while others feel it's undesirable.

The changes in recent years have established many inadequacies related to integrated marketing communications practices. If the challenges of the future must be met, the industry needs to adapt to the changes. The various barriers to IMC process are:

1. **Mindset :** The mind-set that has been built up over the years of practice has rewarded

specialisation and overlooked the need for, and benefits of, integration. Thus, we find that members of the marketing communications industry are not necessarily accepting the concept of integration because their thinking and attitudes are already set against it. Moreover, the query is that what should be integrated? Usually, they do not focus on the spectrum of communication activities and targets; rather they limit their thinking to integration of elements within a single campaign. It is as though they are concerned with 'single battles rather than the whole war'. Integration in true terms takes a wider view.

2. **Structure of Organizations :** The structure of organisations may make it challenging to manage and co-ordinate different specialisms as one entity. Organisations have typically subdivided their tasks into different departments to cope with the magnitude of operations and avoid duplication. Management's response to large, many-faceted tasks has been to disintegrate them and give them to specialists. This applies to marketing communications as well as the task of communicating and co-ordinating is assigned to different departments. On a more negative note, some organisations are scaling down their marketing departments in a belief that marketing has not lived up to its potential.

3. **Elitism :** PR specialists acclaim their dominance over advertising specialists who likewise acclaim their virtues over PR, direct mail and sales promotion, etc. As such views are upheld, it is not likely that specialists will come to the 'promotional discussion table' as equals to decide what is best for the total marketing communications effort of the organization.

4. **Magnitude of Task :** It is challenging to conceptualise the 'Big Picture' and to draft all the organisational influences needed to achieve integration. There are many levels and dimensions of integration which constitute their individual and collective challenges. To be implemented, IMC requires the involvement of its agents and organization.

5. **Adequacy of Budget:** Expenditure on IMC is rarely considered as an investment as most of the organizations fail to recognize the long-term values of marketing communications. Budgets are usually set keeping the short-term perspective in mind rather than long term results. The result is that budgets are lower than those required for the full integration of marketing communications. Many companies fail to invest properly in the development and maintenance of an appropriate database.

6. **Manager Ability :** Cross-disciplinary skills create a barrier to IMC. The skills demanded are wide with few possessing the skills to master them.

CASE STUDY: UNDER ARMOUR-THE NEXT NIKE

Under armour, a Baltimore based company that many have nicknamed as "the next Nike", was founded in 1996 by Kevin Plank, a former Maryland football player who began by selling compression clothing that could "wick" sweat away from body to college sports team out of his car trunk. In 1999, Under Armour received a big break when it was contacted by Warner Brothers for the outfits in two of its feature films. In 2005, the company went public and its stock doubled the very first day while its sales amounted to 606 million US dollars. Under Armour achieved success by focussing on niche market segments that were often overlooked by the customers. The company is known for its great positioning strategy and a unique advertising campaign in 2003, with a theme "protect this house", with a goal to create an advertising spot which lasted longer than 30 seconds. While expanding in 2006 and 2008, it developed a "Click-Clack" campaign while introducing the athletic equipment.

Under Armours integrated marketing communications continue to grow along with the company's sales. The company has a brilliant website where customers can get information about its various products. It has also expanded its sponsorships and has become the official outfitter of a large number of high school and college teams throughout America and now, is competing globally with brand like Nike, Reebok and Adidas. In 2008, the company partnered with ESPN and became the title sponsor of ESPNU High School All- American Game which featured top prep football prospects. Under Armour's success story is just one example on how companies use integrated marketing communications to create awareness and expand their markets.

IMPORTANT QUESTIONS

1. Explain the integrated marketing communication process.
2. Explain briefly various marketing communication tools. What is the significance of each tool?
3. Explain the role of IMC. Also explain the obstacles in implementing IMC.
4. Explain the integrated marketing communication models that assist the IMC process.

❍❍❍

Chapter 6

SALES PROMOTIONS AND PUBLIC RELATIONS

INTRODUCTION

Marketing of products and service these days is incomplete without sales promotion. Sales promotion is a connecting link between personal selling and advertising. Sales promotion covers various other activities which help motivating consumer purchases and dealer effectiveness. Demonstration, trade show, exhibition, exchange offer, seasonal discounts, gifts are popular methods used for promoting sales of the product and demand for service. Since benefits from advertising are reaped in the longerrun, companies therefore invest more in sale promotion in order to get quick results. It involves short-term and add on incentives to the customer for on-the-spot sale of the product.

Those marketing activities other than personal selling, advertising, and publicity that stimulate consumer purchasing and dealer effectiveness, such as display, shows, demonstrations, expositions, and various other non-current selling efforts, not in ordinary routine.

Philip Kotler

Sales promotion consists of a diverse collection of incentive tools, mostly short-term, designed to stimulate quicker and/or greater purchase of particular products/services by consumers or traders.

Robert C. and Scott A.

Sales promotion includes all forms of sponsored communication apart from activities associated with personal selling. It includes trade shows and exhibits, combining, sampling, premiums, trade, allowances, sales and dealer incentives, set of packs, consumer education and demonstration activities, rebates, bonus, packs, point of purchase material and direct mail.

Roger A. Strong

OBJECTIVES OF SALES PROMOTION

The primary goal of sales promotion is to achieve an adjustment in the demand style of items and administration. Essentially, sales promotion has three goals. In the first place, it is intended to give imperative information to the potential buyers. The second goal is to persuade and impact the potential buyers through enticing measures. Thirdly, sales promotion is intended to go about as a ground-breaking instrument of rivalry. The objectives of sales promotion are as per the following:

1. **To introduce new products or services :** Sales promotion is regularly used to spur forthcoming consumers to try new items and services. Merchants are additionally initiated to present new items and services in the market. Generally, free samples are given through merchants amid such presentation. Thus, discounts in cash or merchandise may likewise be offered to retailers to stock new items or manage new services. Free samples, discounts, cash discounts are essentially sales promotion measures.
2. **To attract new customers :** Sales promotion measures also play an important role in attracting new customers for an organization. Usually, new customers are those people that are won away from other firms. Samples, gifts, prizes, etc. are used to encourage consumers to try a new brand or shift their patronage to new dealers.
3. **To encourageexisting customers to buy more :** Sales promotion devices are most often used to induce the existing customers of a firm to buy more. Product development, offering three products at the cost of two, discount coupons, are some of the sales promotion devices used by firms to motivate the existing buyers to buy more of a specific product.
4. **Helps the firm to remain competitive :** Most of the companies undertake sales promotion activities to remain in the competitive market. Therefore, in the modern competitive world no firm can escape the responsibility of undertaking sales promotion activities.

BENEFITS OF SALES PROMOTION

Sales promotion benefits manufacturers, consumers, and traders in a different way. Everyone utilizes the benefit of sales promotion in the way that is most suitable to them.

I. BENEFITS TO THE MANUFACTURERS

1. **Price Differentiation :** Price differentiation can be done by the manufacturers in different cities by adopting different methods of sales promotion. Through exhibitions and stalls, producers can offer price reductions to the customers. Manufacturers use sales promotion to adjust fluctuations in demand and supply of the product without changing the prices of the products.

2. **Trial :** Sales promotion best serves the purpose of the manufacturers when the product is in the testing stage. Sales promotion tool like demonstration is used to induce prospective customers by lowering the costs of perceived risk.

3. **Increase in sales :** Though advertising is also done to increase the sales of the product, sales promotion tools are more effective in increasing the sales in a shorter span of time. Personal selling, gifts, free cards, vouchers etc. help customers to take quicker decisions to purchase the said product or service.

4. **Build a database :** Consumers are required to share their demographic profile like name, address, education, and occupations for receiving promotional offers like coupons, consumer contest and gift cards. These promotional techniques help organizations to gather a personal database for further marketing of their product and service.

5. **Easy to design and implement :** Sales promotion techniques are less expensive as compared to advertising and public relations. Therefore, it becomes easy to design and implement promotional methods both by bigger and smaller organizations.

6. **Useful for small player :** Along with advertising, small players implement promotional techniques to gain a bigger share in the market.

II. BENEFIT TO CONSUMERS

1. **Loyal versus switchers :** It has been observed that people tend to buy things for which they have to pay less. But on the flip side, customers who are loyal to the product will buy even if a slight high price is charged. While the switchers will only buy the product if prices are reduced due to sales promotion.

2. **Price sensitive customers :** Marketers use sales promotional tools to look for price sensitive customers who may switch brands to get price benefits. Customers who are price sensitive also wait for attractive promotional offers from manufacturers to buy durable goods like refrigerators, washing machines etc.

III. BENEFIT TO TRADERS

1. **Forward Buying :** Buying in more quantities provides economies of scale to the purchaser. Retailers buy more during sales season and further provide various promotional offers to increase the sales of the product and service.
2. **New product introduction :** Sales promotion technique helps in promoting the new product in the market which leads to increased sales as customer will prefer buying new products.
3. **Increased store traffic :** Sales promotion techniques like buy one get one free, buy one and get second other at half the price, results in increased store visits by the customers. More store visits results in increased sales to the traders.

DRAWBACKS OF SALES PROMOTION

I. DRAWBACK TO THE MANUFACTURERS

1. **Reduction in brand value :** Frequent sales promotion offers may result in declining brand value. Dominant brand offers not more than 30 percent of the time for sales promotion. Otherwise, there is the risk of declining brand loyalty.
2. **Dilution of quality image :** Too much sales promotion may dilute the importance of the brand image of the product. Customer may perceive hat a particular product is not selling may be due to poor quality.

II. DRAWBACK TO CUSTOMER

Consumers are confused. Too many promotions in identical product categories like televisions or washing machines lead to confusion in the minds of the customers. The decision to choose between brands becomes baffling for the customer.

III. DRAWBACK TO TRADERS

1. **Traders become price sensitive :** Frequent use of trade promotional tools by manufacturers makes traders more price sensitive. A few large retailers demand trade promotions from manufacturers.
2. **Increased competition :** Sales promotion leads to increased competition from intermediaries and increase pressure from manufacturers on the traders to promote the new product and keep a high level of inventory. Traders are messed up in displaying and promoting different brands and at the same time reducing prices.

TYPES OF SALES PROMOTION

Sales promotion efforts are carried out by manufacturers directed towards consumers, traders, business consumers and the sales force. We shall discuss different types of sales promotion to find out the greater details.

I. CONSUMERS PROMOTIONS

Also known as sales promotion is directed towards consumers both individual as well as organizations. Sales Promotion supplements by providing additional incentives to both the consumer markets as well as business markets in order toencourage them to buy the product. Consumer promotions help in pushing up purchase of larger size units. It also entices brand switchers to try the product by offering it at reduced prices. Consumer promotions have short term influence on the consumers; hence the promotions should be made in collaboration with integrated marketing communication (IMC) plan to make them more enticing and effective. Some major types of consumer promotions are as follows:

1. SAMPLES

Under this method, the producer distributes free samples of his product among the consumers. Sales representatives distribute these samples door-to-door. This method is used mostly in the case of products of daily-use, e.g. Washing Powder, Tea, Toothpaste, etc. Thus, the consumers willy-nilly make use of free samples. If it satisfies them, they buy it and in this way sales are increased.

S. No	Common ways	Places where samples are distributed
1.	In-Store Distribution	Retail Outlets
2.	Direct Sampling	Residence of customers sent either by post or delivered directly
3.	Response Sampling	Made available to individuals, households & business organizations who respond to media offers
4.	Media Sampling	Sample is included in media outlet. For example, a small sample of shampoo attached in a magazine
5.	Selective Sampling	Samples are distributed at a site like trade fair, sporting event or hospital

Though sales promotion by sampling method is effective in the case of the new product but it does not provide assurance that the customer will actually buy the product. Sampling is also an expensive method of promotion.

It is predominantly used in the FMCG industry for perfumes, deodorants, soaps or even eatables.

2. COUPONS

They are certificates that offer reduction in price to the buyers when they purchase specified products. These can be mailed, included with other products, or placed in ads. They can be usedin kind or cash. These are most popular in the restaurant industry; however, hotel, rental car companies, tourists' attractions, and cruise lines also use coupons.

S. No.	Types of coupons	Position	Redemption
1.	Instant redemption Coupon	Placed in package or distributed in retail outlets	Redeemed for purchase of additional packages of product and for trial of new purchases
2.	Scanned Delivered Coupons	Placed at cash register	Redeemed on brand switching when the item is scanned as a reduction in price
3.	Bounce Back Coupons	Placed inside packages	Redeemed on repeat purchase.
4.	Cross Ruffling	Placed inside package of another product	Products purchased and consumed at same time. For example Britannia industry may place coupon of butter on package of bread.
5.	Response Offer	Issued on request by customers	These coupons can be used for both household and business customers on request

Coupons help in boosting the sales of the product, but they can be easily used to redeem fraudulently at fraudulent retail shops. Still, coupons are frequently used by the consumers because buyers find them more attractive, higher face value and free standing inserts which give them freedom to choose a particular coupon at their home.

3. PREMIUMS OR GIFTS

Premiums are goods offered either free or at low cost as an incentive to buy a product. Promotional items such as caps, T-shirts, and sweatshirts can be sold at a good profit, thus creating another profit center for the company. Others offer a premium-priced drink or dessert that is served with a special glass or plate. Guests actually pay for the glass or plate in the price of the product, take the "gift" home with them, and are reminded of a pleasant restaurant experience each time it is later seen

S. No.	Premium	Nature
1.	In- or on-package premium	These are small gifts inside the package. For example, a coffee mug free with Nescafe packing
2.	Free in the mail premiums	Gifts are received after providing proof to the manufacturer of the purchase of the product
3.	Self-liquidating premiums	Gift is offered for which consumer pays the cost and shipping charges after showing proof of purchase
4.	Store or manufacturing premiums	Gifts are given by the manufacturer or retailer when the customer purchases the product. For example, an autographed photo of Sachin Tendulkar with purchase of Boost and a skipping rope for school children

Premiums are valuable offers for the manufacturers and retailers if premium gifts match the perception of the target audience. Moreover the premium should be related to the company's product and product should be of superior quality. A low-class product with no use as a premium would demotivate consumers to buy the product on repeat purchase.

4. CONTEST AND SWEEPSTAKES (PRIZES)

Some producers organize contests with a view to popularizing their products. Consumers taking part in the contest are asked to answer some very simple questions like completion of a slogan or a sentence which may say, "I like the product of brand X because________, "I like commercial of product Y because____ on a form and forward the same to the company. The blank form is made available to that consumer who buys the product first. The result is declared by the panel of judges on the basis of all the forms received by a particular date. Attractive prizes are given to the winners of the contest. Such contests can be organized in different ways. A sweepstakes calls for consumers to submit their names for a drawing. The customer does not have to purchase the product. The companies restrict the entry to one person for the sweepstakes. Consumers get many opportunities to win prizes by participating in different contests and sweepstakes. Assurance of instant winning increases the interest of the consumers to indulge themselves in the challenging games. The main problem linked with such offerings is lack of interest from customers and huge expenditure involved.

5. REFUND AND REBATES

Refunds are a marketing tactic when you get a partial amount refunded to you based on an action you have taken. For example – if you bring the parking ticket to the showroom, your parking amount will be refunded by the store. Such refunds make the customer excited to visit a store. Similarly, a rebate is a type of partial refund which is widely used for consumer durables like automobiles, television and computer, which are hard goods. In rebates, you fill forms while checking out of stores. Rebates are normally higher in value. Manufactures should make the refund and rebate program more reachable to the consumers by using advertising campaigns.

6. PRICE-OFFS

Price-offs are promotional offerings given to stimulate the sales of the product and motivate consumers to buy the product in larger quantities. Price offs as the name suggests is a temporary price reduction to consumers. These offers help the companies to increase the sale for the temporary period but reduces long term profits. Too much dependence on price offs can damage the company's brand image and may force consumers to switch to other brands.

7. BONUS PACKS

A bonus pack is a manufacturer's sales promotion technique of giving the buyer an extra quantity of a product at the usual price (e.g., an extra 6 oz free; buy four, get one free). This gives consumers more value for money. Bonus packs are strong influences and can prevent a competitor's promotion strategies. Bonus packs are considered as a reward for customer loyalty. Sometimes, consumers might get dicey about the bonus offers associated with the product like buy one get one free, on purchase of two by the third free. The consumer may not perceive it as value for money. This may raise the question of the brand image in the market. Therefore, the manufacturer must be extra conscious before announcing any bonus packs with the product.

8. EVENT MARKETING

Under event marketing company becomes the part of specific event and includes some type of tangible presence, such as display booth at the event. Various events like sporting events, musical concerts, fashion, and modeling contests are organized to market the products and services in the market. In India, Times of India group initiated "Femina Miss India Contest" and "Lakme Fashion Week" which is examples of event marketing. Event Sponsorship- Company provides financial support for the event and in return got its brand name displayed in the event. The name is displayed as an advertisement or as a logo. Many big industrialists like reliance Jio group is the major sponsor of Filmfare awards, Sahara Group in India is the sponsor of Indian Cricket team for several years. The company names are displayed prominently on the screen.

Event marketing agencies like Nimbus and Madison have mastered in sport events and Wizcraft International in glamorous events such as film star awards and beauty contests.

9. FREQUENCY (OR LOYALTY) PROGRAMMES

Loyalty or frequency programs are a unique type of sales promotion in that they have a long-term focus. Most sales promotions are intended to create near-term sales. Loyalty programs are ongoing incentives to loyal customers who purchase at certain levels. Typically, customers receive points or bonus coupons when they reach certain spending increments. Frequent-flier airline programs and hotel rewards are examples.

Event marketing and event sponsorship- Such promotional tools have gained much hype for customer-oriented promotions to increase the sales by the companies. Though, these are two different terms often used interchangeably.

10. POINT-OF-PURCHASE DISPLAYS (POP)

Point-of-sale displays are sales promotions that are placed where they can easily draw customer attention and trigger impulse buying. A point-of-purchase or POP display is marketing material or advertising placed next to the merchandise it is promoting. These items are generally located in the checkout area or other location where the purchase decision is made. More commonly abbreviated to POP by retailers, this can be one of the most underutilized tools in retail. POP displays can be as simple as a sign or as elaborate as a display carton. For example, a retailer may use a "shelf talker" (a sticker stuck to the end of the shelf to draw attention as the customer walks down the aisle of a grocery store) which is a small visual item. Or they may create a full display where the vendor's products are merchandised inside it. Think of a free-standing display with the vendor's branding on it, with only its merchandise on display inside.

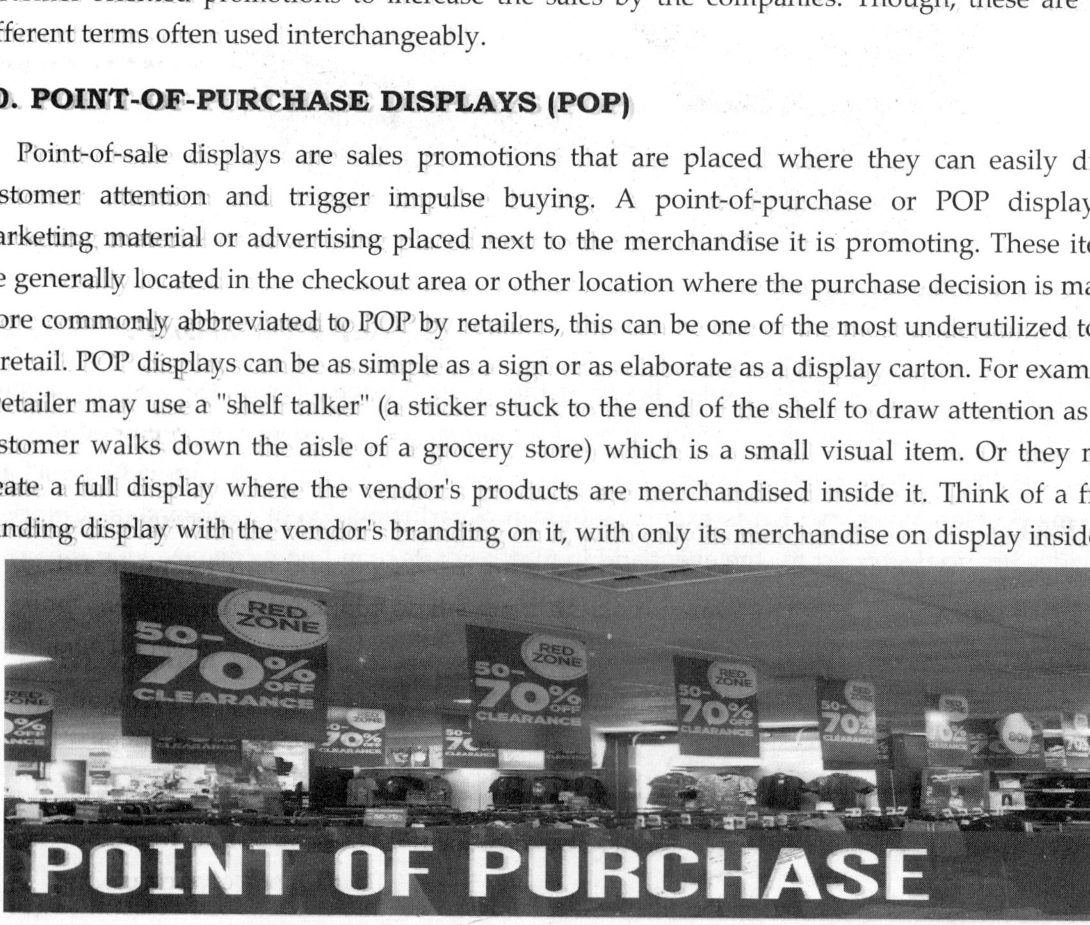

II. TRADE PROMOTIONS

Trade promotions are part of the push strategy of the manufacturers. Manufactures want to rid themselves of the huge expenditure on promotions. Therefore, they want to obtain some benefits by offering trade promotions to re-sellers. The trade promotions are directed at re-sellers, such as distributors, wholesalers, dealers, and retailers.

TYPES OF TRADE PROMOTION

1. TRADE CONTESTS

Dealers, retailers, or retail salespeople are offered trade contest in help achieving sales goal of the manufacturer. The manufacturer provides monetary rewards to the retailer, dealer, and salespeople for selling the manufacturer's goods. The rewards can also be in kind such as television, washing machines or stereos. Such rewards in cash or kind are known as push money or spiff money. These benefits are given to traders when they sale the manufacturer's brand over the other competing brands. Trade contests work well if they are restricted to few specific dealers.

2. TRAINING PROGRAMMES

Training is an essential managerial function which helps to improve the working skill of the individuals. Different training programmes for salespeople of retailers and dealers are organized by the manufacturer. Advanced information about the product features, benefits, advantages over competing brands is provided to salespeople at the location of retailers. This training is given by the manufacturers' own salespeople as they meet retail staff during their regular visit to a retailer or dealer. The advanced and updated information helpssalespeople of the retailer to sell more of the manufacturer product. Sometimes the manufacturer provides video cassettes, product brochures and relevant material to the salespeople so that they can answer the queries of the customers.

3. TRADE SHOWS

Trade shows and exhibitions can be an excellent way to promote your business and the products and services that you offer. They are also a great way to network with other industry members and grow your customer base. A trade show is an event where goods and services in a specific industry are exhibited and demonstrated to other businesses. An exhibition is the same, except the audience is normally the public. The members (Manufacturers or suppliers) participating in the trade show are required to buy a space to set up their booth, arrange displays and demonstrations of the product. Trade shows invite huge numbers of public as well as business customers. Trade shows benefits the most in introducing new products, followed by identifying prospective customers, meeting existing customers and increasing sales. Manufacturers of household furniture, tiles, and bathroom fittings have booths in the trade shows.

4. COOPERATIVE ADVERTISING

Cooperative advertising is the sharing of costs for locally placed advertising between a retailer or wholesaler and a manufacturer. Many manufacturers have a set amount of cooperative advertising funds available per year, distributed as opportunities for collaboration arise. Manufacturers report, however, that much of this money goes unspent, as relatively few retailers and wholesalers pursue cooperative agreements. There are three types of cooperative advertising out of which only vertical cooperative advertising is used as a promotional tool for trade.

S. No.	Cooperative Advertising	Meaning
1.	Horizontal	In this type, two or more types of retailers/franchisees share the costs. A horizontal cooperative advertising agreement helps the parties endorse the same product. For example, a coaching center has its franchisees spread across various geographical locations. However, the advertisement is under the same banner, and the costs are shared by all the franchisees.
2.	Vertical	In this type, advertisement costs are shared by retailers and manufacturers/wholesalers (those who appear earlier than the retailer in the chain). Example of a vertical cooperative advertising: A retail outlet of Walmart advertises products of their manufacturers.
3.	Ingredient-Sponsored	This advertising is encouraged by manufacturers of raw material and component parts. One of the most successful examples is "Intel Inside". It offers a cooperative fund to all PC makers that place Intel logo on their computers.

5. TRADE ALLOWANCES

A trade allowance is when manufacturers give retailers an allowance or a refund on their products. In exchange the retailer agrees to promote the manufacturer's products within their stores. The types of trade allowances used by manufacturer are as follows:

S. No.	Trade Allowances	Meaning
1.	Off-invoice Allowance	It is a discount offered to members in a form of an invoice or it can be taken as a form of free goods or extra goods taken with purchase of specific number of goods

2.	Slotting Allowance	This allowance is paid by the manufacturer to the retailer for managing the new product. Retailers charge such allowance to cover their inventory carrying cost, rearranging of shelf space, and deleting of other products.
3.	Promotional Allowance	These allowances are given for advertising manufacturers' products or brand, arranging special displays, and carrying out promotional programmes in retail outlets. These allowances are given as discount on listed price or as a fixed amount for specific products.
4.	Drop-Ship Allowance	This allowance is paid when retailers directly make a relationship with the manufacturer when orders are placed. Shorter supply chain helps in increasing the savings of the customers, but it may result in unsatisfactory relationship with wholesaler and distributor.
5.	Exit Fees	This allowance is paid as substitute of slotting allowance. As the retailer deletes the older product for introducing new product of the retailer, manufacturer is required to pay certain monetary allowance to the trader.

OTHER ACTION ORIENTED ADVERTISING

1. **Retail Advertising :** Retail advertising is when stores use ads to make people want to come to their store and buy things. The best retail ads give a lot of details about what they are selling, like the colors, sizes, and prices of the products. It's not enough to just say the products are available in different colors and sizes; it's better to list the exact options and prices. Missing information can stop people from taking action. Retail ads also try to create a sense of urgency by saying that the products are available at special prices for a limited time. For big items like appliances and cars, the goal of advertising might be to get people to visit the store in person. When it comes to selling expensive things, it's often better to have salespeople talk to customers in the store, and advertising is used to get people to visit the store.

2. **Cooperative Advertising :** Cooperative advertising is when a manufacturer helps stores with their advertising. They might give suggestions on how to make ads, provide materials to create the ads, and even contribute money to cover some of the costs. It also involves stores stocking certain amounts of the manufacturer's products and using specific displays. About half of retail advertising is some form of cooperative advertising. The main goal of cooperative advertising is usually to boost short-term

sales. Ads are good for this because they give specific information about the product, where to buy it, and how much it costs. But cooperative advertising also has longer-term goals like building up the manufacturer's brand image and maintaining a strong relationship between the manufacturer and the stores.

3. **Reminder, Point-of-Purchase, and Specialty Advertising :** Sometimes, the main job of advertising is to remind people to buy a certain brand. This is usually when the brand is already well-known and trusted. Reminder ads are meant to make people think about buying the brand when they are shopping. They can work in different ways, like making sure people remember the brand when they make their shopping list or buy something on impulse. To do this, reminder ads might be short and shown often, like quick 15-second commercials, or they might use media like billboards or ads in stores to catch people's attention when they're shopping.

   Point of Purchase displays, often abbreviated as POP displays, are promotional materials and advertising tools placed near the checkout area or other strategic locations within a retail store. Their primary purpose is to attract the attention of shoppers and encourage impulse purchases or promote specific products or brands.

   Specialty advertising, also known as promotional products or promotional items, refers to branded merchandise that companies give away or sell to promote their brand, products, or services. These items typically feature a company's logo, slogan, or contact information and serve as tangible reminders of the brand.

4. **In-Store Advertising and Merchandising :** In-store advertising is getting more popular because marketers know that most people decide what to buy once they are inside a store. So, they use different types of ads inside stores to get people to notice their products. This can include electronic ads on screens in the aisles, ads on TVs near the checkout, or even ads on shopping carts with video screens. Some of these new advertising methods have been very successful, but others have had problems because it's hard to measure how well they work.

PUBLIC RELATIONS (PR)

PR is used by companies to talk about themselves in a way that doesn't look like advertising. This is because people try to avoid ads and often don't trust them. To reach people who are hard to reach and make them believe in their message, companies use PR alongside advertising. PR can involve getting their name in newspapers or magazines or sponsoring events. It's mainly used to make people like the company or fix a bad image.

Tata Group's Global Acquisitions: The Tata Group, a well-known Indian conglomerate, has made several global acquisitions in the past. Tata Motors' acquisition of Jaguar Land Rover in

2008 was a significant PR moment for the brand. Tata Group used PR to showcase how this acquisition would benefit both the brand and the British automotive industry. They focused on preserving the legacy of these iconic brands while integrating them into the Tata family.

Coca-Cola's "Share a Coke" Campaign: Coca-Cola India launched a PR campaign called "Share a Coke," where they replaced their logo with popular Indian names on their bottles. This personalized approach was a hit in India and generated significant media coverage and social media buzz. It allowed consumers to connect with the brand on a personal level.

Types of PR in Marketing:

1. **News Stories and Media Editorial Coverage:** Some companies get their top executives to write articles in magazines to show that they are leaders in their industry.
2. **Event and Sports Marketing:** This means promoting products during sports events or with the help of famous athletes or sports teams. It can also involve promoting sports themselves or using them to help with marketing efforts. This can be really effective, especially during big sporting events when a lot of people are interested.
3. **Cause-Related Marketing:** This is when a company partners with a charity to support a good cause. For example, a company might donate a portion of their profits from a product to an animal shelter. This way, the company not only helps the charity but also improves its own image.
4. **Product Placement:** Product development is the process of turning an idea into a product that can be sold. It involves many steps, like research, development,

manufacturing, and distribution. Product development is important to make sure the product is valuable to customers and meets high-quality standards. The best products also help society improve, either through the product itself or by creating jobs and income.

IMPORTANT QUESTIONS

1. Explain with advantages and disadvantages of various sales promotion tools and techniques.
2. What are the merits and demerits of sales promotion?
3. What do you understand by PR? Explain with examples.
4. What are modern action oriented types of advertising?

❍ ❍ ❍

Chapter 7

SETTING GOALS AND OBJECTIVES

INTRODUCTION

Perhaps one of the reasons why companies fail to establish objectives for their integrated marketing communications is that they don't recognize the value of doing so. Another reason may be disagreement as to what specific objectives should be. However, marketing objectives are needed in an organization as they serve the purpose of planning, decision making, budget formation, measurement, and evaluation of results. The marketing objectives must be set after thorough situational analysis with proper media and message strategy to achieve the desired results.

MODELS FOR MARKETING COMMUNICATION

Marketing communication models emerged because of various studies that explain how communications work in marketing a product. They act as indispensable tools in understanding how communications work in real life marketing situations and for developing a communication strategy. Communication strategy can make or break a brand by fabricating an image or perception in the mind of customers positively and they may make a purchase.

The models of marketing communications are: -

(1) DAGMAR

(2) AIDA model

(3) DRIP model

DAGMAR

DAGMAR approach of advertising was devised by Mr. Russell Colley in 1961 in a report to the Association of National Advertisers. Colley advised that effective advertising seeks to communicate rather than sell. His work is appreciated till date, as many companies use DAGMAR concept to set advertising objectives and goals. DAGMAR is an acronym for "**Defining advertising goals for measured advertising results**". Advertisers discover whether their message conveyed enough information and understanding of a product to their consumers and its respective benefits from clear objectives.

The 2 important things on which the DAGMAR Model stood were:

- Creation of a communication task to achieve goals.
- Defining the objective of the communication tasks in a manner that the results can be measured.

A. Communication task

It is a marketing tool to enumerate the results of an advertising campaign. DAGMAR seeks to guide customers through ACCA approach. According to this approach, every purchase encounter four steps; Awareness, Comprehension, Conviction, and Action:

- **Awareness** – Communication tasks associated with making the consumer aware of the brand or the product.
- **Comprehension** – These tasks also aided the consumer in understanding the features and the attributes of the product and what the product will do for the consumer.
- **Conviction** – The communication task persuaded the consumer that this product was meant for them.
- **Action** – Ultimately, after conviction, the customer was to be tempted to act.

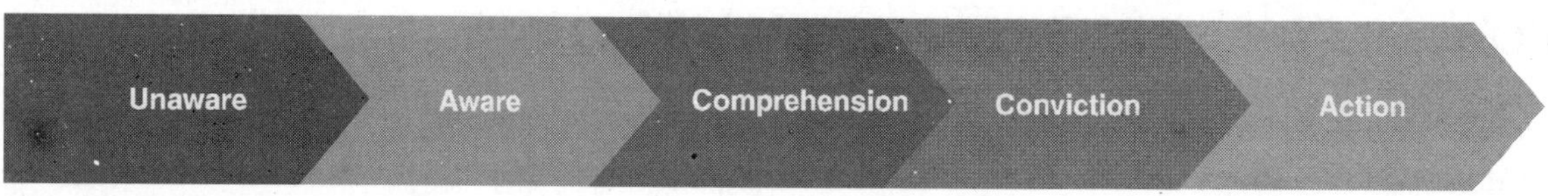

B. Defining objectives in the DAGMAR approach

Following the communication task is the job of defining measurable objectives. The issue does not end at just designing the communication task. Because designing this task is very difficult if the objectives of advertising are not known. If you don't know WHY you are communicating to the customer, then how will you communicate? Thus, DAGMAR then also included defining the Objectives for communications. Colley developed a checklist of 52 advertising tasks to serve as a starting point for establishing objectives.

The objectives of advertising in DAGMAR (which are used to design communication tasks) are as follows:

1. **Concrete and measurable tasks :** The communications task or objective should be an unambiguous and precise statement of what appeal or message the advertiser wants to communicate to the target market. Furthermore, the specification should include specifications of the measurement procedure. Does he want to build the brand image, maximise the brand presence, infiltrate new markets or increase overall sales?

   For example: Foster's Beer saw a sales decline after a successful introduction. Knowing that something had to be done soon, they developed a set of objectives as guidelines for future like:

   - Strengthen brand's image
   - Maximize brand's market share and presence
   - Increase sales

   Using a combination of variety of marketing media to create brand awareness along with specified tasks helped foster beer to increase its sale by 12.1%.

   Thus, there must be a way to communicate the tasks so that they can be measured properly.

2. **Target audience :** Target market is the group of potential customers or clients. These customers have the highest possibility of purchasing the product. The identification process includes geographic, demographic, and psychographic segmentation. The targeted market may be narrow or broad depending on marketing initiatives and sales goals. Target markets can be separated into primary and secondary groups. Primary markets are members of the target audience, to which marketing efforts are primarily focused. Secondary markets are the target audience members that marketing efforts will be directed after the primary market is reached.

   Example: The target audience of Dior is: females of 25 years and above, high social status having high income. Once this has been established, it is easier to allocate advertising budgets for different media for creating brand awareness among the target audience. Thus, it is essential for establishing an effective positioning strategy.

3. **Benchmark and degree of change sought :** Another important part of setting objectives is having benchmark measures to determine where the target audience stands at the starting of the campaign with respect to various communication response variables such as awareness, knowledge, attitudes, image, etc. A benchmark is also a precondition to the ultimate measurement of results, an essential part of any planning program and DAGMAR. If we could first know where we are and what we are tending, we could achieve it in a better way.

What level of attitude, perception, or awareness of the customer do you want to change? If a customer is aware of the product, do you want his negative attitude to change to positive? Or if the market is completely unaware, do you want the whole market to be aware or only partially the target group itself? These degrees of change which are going to be the objective of the communication task need to be defined in advance.

An advertisement campaign which generates 90% brand awareness cannot be judged as effective until and unless one knows what percentage of consumers were aware of the product before the ad campaign.

4. **Specified time period :** A good objective has a specified time frame, during which the objective is to be achieved. Understanding the specifications enables advertisers to define goals that will give the best results. That's why major advertisers try to introduce the product for 3 months, and then communicate the features and benefits for the next 3 months so that the brand recall is high and the brand acceptance is high as well. A defined time period gives better measurability.

   Example: Repositioning of Marlboro from a feminine to masculine brand took several years.

5. **Written :** The goal should be committed on a paper. When the goals are clearly written, basic shortfalls and flaws are exposed, ultimately it becomes easy to determine whether the goal contains the important aspects of the DAGMAR approach.

CRITICISMS OF DAGMAR

DAGMAR has some limitations too:

- **Problems with the response hierarchy :** Dependence on traditional hierarchical type response models (ACCA) is a drawback in the original version of DAGMAR. This is because an individual may focus on benefits of the products first and features later or vice versa. This makes the ACCA approach of DAGMAR unnecessary.
- **Problems with attitude-behaviour relationship :** Some criticize DAGMAR since it implies that movement through the hierarchy will result to changes in attitudes and succeeding behaviour. Since the ACCA approach is not effective, the attitude and ultimately behaviour cannot be changed. Also, there are problems with the assumption that attitudes are related to behaviour. Apart from this, the attitude and behaviour is difficult to measure.
- **Sales objectives :** Supporters of sales objectives argue that communication objectives advocated by DAGMAR are a "cop-out" and a way of ignoring the fundamental goal of advertising which is to create and increase sales. They argue that since a communication

objective is of interest only if it can be shown to be related to sales, why not simply use sales as the objective?

- **Practicality and costs :** DAGMAR is criticized for being too complicated to implement and practical only for big companies with large marketing and advertising research budgets who can afford to establish quantitative benchmarks and measure communication results.
- **Inhibits creativity :** DAGMAR is also criticized on the grounds that it can restrict creativity by imposing too much influence or structure on creativity. The creative department may become too concerned with "passing the numbers test" rather than developing great ideas that result in eccentric and effective advertising. Many advertising people have blamed the lack of great creative ideas and campaigns in the U.S. in recent years on an over quantification of advertising objectives.

DAGMAR II

The criticisms of DAGMAR led to development of improved model, known as DAGMAR II. This model is more analytical and accurate as it gives importance to attitude, perception and behaviour of consumer. This is a situational model which takes into consideration different situations and variables.

AIDA model

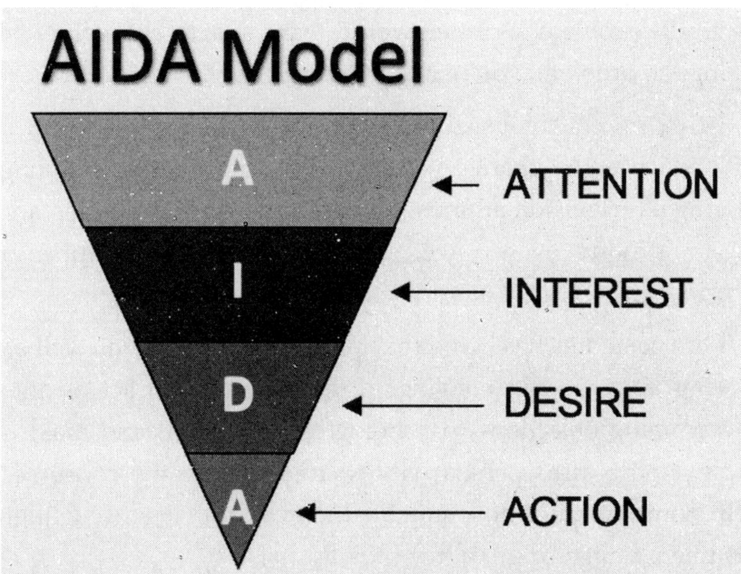

AIDA was introduced by an American businessman; E. St. Elmo Lewis in 1898, predominantly addressing the optimization of sales calls. In the model, he specifically referred to the interaction between marketer and customer concerning the product. As an abbreviation,

AIDA breaks down into the steps required for successful marketing: Attention, Interest, Desire and Action. The AIDA marketing model is a centrepiece of modern marketing, to the extent that missing one step is thought to almost guarantee a failed result.

The simplest yet most powerful formula has following steps:

1. **Attention :** Often, the attention part is ignored by many marketers. It is assumed that the product or service already got the attention of the consumers – which may or may not be the case. In any event, it is illogical to presume that everyone is aware of your product. One of the best approaches to attracting consumer attention is what's called "creative disruption" – breaking current patterns of behaviour through a highly creative message. This can be done in several ways:

   - Placing advertisements in uncommon situations or locations. This is often referred to as guerrilla marketing.
   - Creating shockvertising through provoking imagery.
   - An intensely targeted message. This is known as personalization.

   Essentially, the goal is to make consumers aware that a product or service exists.

2. **Interest :** Once you've gained the prospects' attention, the next step is to sustain interest in your product or service to keep the beneficiaries engaged. Explain to the beneficiaries how the problem you've identified in the attention step is adversely affecting their lives. A demonstration or illustration can help the beneficiaries to further identify with the problem and they would want to actively seek possible solutions. By personalizing the problem, you're making it hit closer to home.

3. **Desire :** There's an enormous difference between being interested in something and desiring it. You need to change your viewer's interest into a strong desire for what you're offering. A television ad must generate a strong motivation and generate a need for buying the product even if need is not there. This will happen only if the ad has used the correct appeal in the advertisement.

4. **Action :** If the customer has come this far, there is interest as well as desire. The final step is closing the sale and convincing the customer to act on interest, which may involve overcoming objections (psychological or logical) and making a call to action. For example, Netflix uses persuasive text to persuade the consumer to try their free trial. Netflix communicates how suitable their product is and highlights its value, then urges consumers to sign up for a free trial.

   Good advertising should induce a sense of urgency that drives consumers to take action RIGHT NOW. One commonly used method for achieving this goal is making limited time offers (such as: buy 1, get 1 free, product combinations, and free shipping).

CRITICISMS OF AIDA MODEL

For a long time, the AIDA model was viewed as exemplary for a successful sales process, but today there is general agreement that using this purely linear model alone is no longer suitable in modern sales processes.

- The step-by-step model provides a relatively fixed sequence of individual steps. In practice, however, a sales process does not always have to be linear. For example, the stages "Attraction" and "Interest" can be completed as one phase. In addition, various media and/or devices can be used in the course of the customer journey until an interested party becomes a buyer. A simple AIDA step-by-step model does not take these different paths to the goal into account. This is why non-hierarchical multi-process models are mostly used today in advertising impact research.
- The emotion that is often addressed in advertising does not play a role in the AIDA formula. Targeting and, for example, considerations on socio-demographic background is also not included. AIDA also does not consider the different points at which sales take place. The sales strategy for a customer visiting an online shop will be quite different to that for new a customer wanting to find out about a new car at the dealership.
- You need to know AIDA is too simplistic to describe the stages of a complex buying process, particularly for decisions that are more involved or nuanced. Nowadays, consumers have a lot of different ways they can research, compare products, etc.

VARIANTS OF AIDA

Modified AIDA Model:

Awareness→ Interest→Conviction →Desire→ Action (purchase or consumption)

This variant on AIDA includes a 'C' for *Conviction*. The proposition is that before you get to a final purchase action, a cognitive state of understanding the value is needed that matches the emotional state of desire. This may appear before Desire (AICDA) or after Desire (AIDCA), possibly showing two different approaches: one which starts with getting a logical agreement and then moving to emotional desire, as opposed to creating desire first and then reaching the state when the purchase makes logical sense.

AIDAS Model:

Attention → Interest → Desire → Action → Satisfaction

The letter 'S' for satisfaction also gets added (AIDAS), indicating the fact that happy and satisfied customers would buy more and also, refer the products or services to their social groups.

AIDAL

AIDA + L, for loyalty: According to this approach, the sale does not end with a one-off transaction but instead focuses on its regularity and repeatability. And this is where the loyalty mentioned above comes in handy, which makes prospects come back and make more purchases.

DRIP MODEL

Bowersox and Morash (1989) demonstrated how marketing flows, including the information flow, can be represented as a system whose sole purpose is the satisfaction of customer needs and wants. Communication plays a crucial role in these exchange networks. At a basic level, communication can bear one of four main roles:

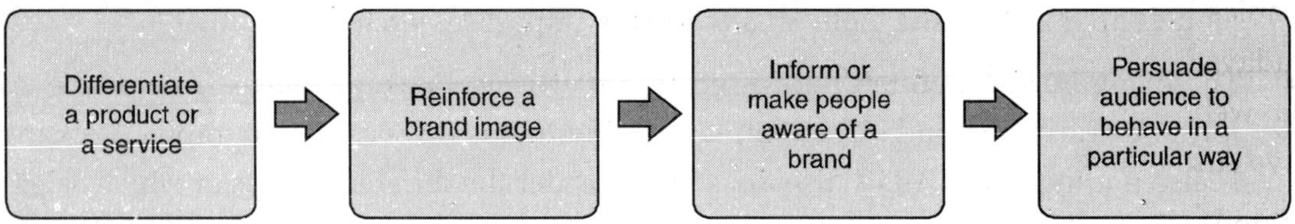

1. Differentiate

Here, companies differentiate their product/services from others of same product class. Though it is demanding but it can be done by understanding how your product is positioned in the market. The aim here is to originate liking for the product among the target audience from the pool of other similar products. Usually, 7 P's of marketing are used for this purpose.

For example, in the comparative ads between Pepsodent and Colgate, Pepsodent differentiates itself by claiming to have 130% germ killing potential which is more than 100% that of Colgate. This differentiation on the grounds of efficacy develops liking for Pepsodent.

2. Reinforce

Here the goal is to remind the customers of the benefits of a product or persuade them to start a new negotiation. Companies can describe their brand as an experience encased in a promise and reinforce the brand's message. Reinforcement can be attained via demonstrating experiences. Such demonstrations should depict why your product is superior or how it is different from others. There may be cognitive dissonance in the minds of consumers, and they may have many objections so, there is a need to create a reminder for the products.

For instance, Amitabh Bachchan respectfully describes how family bond never breaks, reinforcing the brand message "Sadiyonkeliye" of Binani Cement.

3. Inform

As simple as its name, companies inform about offering or make the target group aware about it. They communicate and educate about their offerings to their prospects. This may include new features, benefits, offers, value, availability, etc. This will educate the consumer about the product.

Fogg perfume gives 800 sprays. This more usage feature is well transmitted to the customers. Now the customer is well aware about your product, and he has some knowledge about it. This will also increase Top-of-the-mind awareness.

4. Persuade

It means instigate your prospect to behave in a certain way. Companies persuade their target audience to behave in a particular way, which evokes certain attitude within customers. Here companies build a relationship with the customers, getting into emotional connect with them. Nowadays it is so easy to get in touch with the customers. Talk about the product on social media websites, engage with customers on social media, and offerfree trials to encourage positive customer behaviour.

Hippo via it's Save hunger campaign connects with its consumers on twitter. The consumer just needs to tweet at hippo twitter handle @Myhippo and hippo is made available at nearby shops. This element evokes action-oriented behaviour such as trial purchase.

Here is an example of how Starbucks could apply DRIP to promote their products.

- **Differentiate**: Starbucks maintains its edge over its competitors by selling their product in 75 markets and also, claims to serve 87000 different drink combinations. The coffee giant focuses on drive-thru's rather than opening a dine-in restaurant.
- **Reinforce**: To reinforce the brand message, Starbucks treats its employees as partners and offers them stock options and health insurances. They also create a relaxed

environment for the customers, and this stands true to their mission statement: "To inspire and nurture the human spirit – one person, one cup and one neighbourhood at a time".

- **Inform**: To inform people about the brand, Starbucks encourages social interactions with the bloggers and the same is informed through social media platforms like twitter, facebook or their own website i.e. www.starbucks.in
- **Persuade:** To persuade the customers they started many Twitters campaign #TweetACoffee, #AwesomeThursdays to create awareness about their products and campaigns like #UnconditionalPride was initiated to create awareness about gender equality.

Advantages

Advantages include the automation and efficiency, as well as sustaining ability for direct response. E-commerce sites, such as Dell, have integrated this form of drip campaign with un-purchased shopping carts. The continued messaging is relevant to the contents that the shopper stopped short of purchasing, and continued to include direct response actions (i.e. buy now).

Disadvantages

Disadvantages include the impersonal manner of follow-up. If not augmented with a traditional and personal follow-up method, this automated follow-up has a lower response rate than does personal sales. The lowered response rate is often justified by the volume and efficiency with which leads can be generated and converted.

BEHAVIOURAL DYNAMICS

An understanding of market dynamics is necessary to an analysis of the ultimate behaviour on which advertising should focus. An increase in sales or, more generally, an increase in product use (if the advertiser were a library or hospital or credit card company, a sales measure would be inappropriate) can basically come from various sources: from new customers attracted to the brand for the first time, by increasing the loyalty of existing customers, and by inducing existing customers to use more of the product class, either by increased usage or in new situations. It involves:

- **Segment E:** These are people who buy our brand, but they might also buy other brands sometimes because they don't really mind which brand they use. Some of them use our brand for some things and other brands for different things.
- **Segment 0**: These people only buy other brands and never choose our brand. Some might stick to one brand, while others switch between brands.

- **Segment N:** These people don't buy any brand from this product category. They don't use these products at all, like not drinking coffee or not using computers.

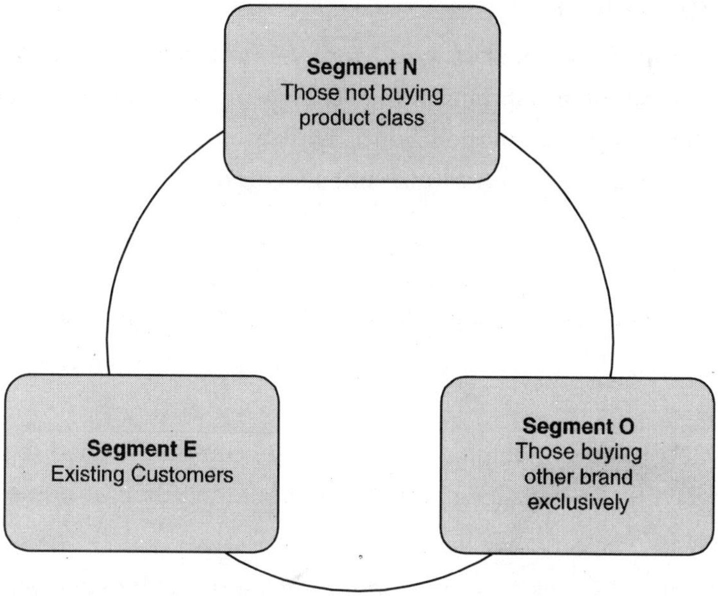

1. **Attracting Customers from Other Brands:** The goal is to get more people to use our brand (Segment E). We can do this by convincing people from Segment 0 (who use other brands) to try ours. We can also target customers from competing brands that are likely to buy more of our product in the future or are more profitable for us. Sometimes, we focus on people who can influence others to switch to our brand. For example, Nike tries to get coaches to wear their shoes because it influences athletes and fans.

2. **Attracting Customers from Different Product Categories:** Instead of convincing people who already use similar products (Segment 0), we try to get people who don't use our type of product at all (Segment N). For example, Pepsi might try to get young coffee drinkers to switch to Pepsi in the morning instead of coffee.

3. **Increasing How Much People Buy:** Some customers switch between different brands. They don't stick to just one. We can try to make these customers more loyal to our brand. If our brand has advantages they don't know about, we can tell them. But if they think all brands are the same, it's hard and might cost a lot. We need to balance the cost with the benefit.

4. **Making Customers Loyal and Preventing Them from Leaving:** We're not the only ones advertising. Our competitors also try to steal our customers. So, we need to keep our current customers happy and prevent them from trying other brands. For example, if our brand has a lot of people leaving (low repurchase rate), we should try to stop

them from leaving. We don't want them to switch to another brand. Sometimes, we're also worried about customers moving from using our brand (Segment E) to not using any brand (Segment N).

5. **Getting Existing Customers to Use More:** Some brands are already leaders in their product categories, like Campbell Soup. They want their customers to use more of their product. For example, Campbell Soup, with a big share of the soup market, wants people to have soup not just for lunch but also for dinner.

Recent Examples:

In recent years, smartphone companies like Apple and Samsung have been trying to attract customers from other brands by introducing new features and designs with each new phone release.

- During the COVID-19 pandemic, many beverage companies tried to attract people who used to drink coffee at cafes (Segment N) by marketing their at-home coffee products as a replacement for cafe coffee.
- Streaming services like Netflix work on increasing usage by suggesting new shows and movies based on what users have watched before, keeping them engaged and watching more.
- Brands use social media to reinforce loyalty by engaging with customers and showing them why their brand is special, like sharing behind-the-scenes content or customer stories.
- Companies like Amazon use a defensive strategy by offering loyalty programs like Amazon Prime to keep customers from switching to competitors.

IMPORTANT QUESTIONS

1. Explain in detail the marketing communication models.
2. Write short notes on:
   (a) AIDA
   (b) DRIP
3. Discuss the term DAGMAR. Explain the characteristics of advertising objectives given in DAGMAR approach. What are the criticisms of the model?
4. What do you understand by Behavioural dynamics? Explain in detail.

❍❍❍

Chapter 8

FACILITATING AGENCIES

INTRODUCTION

Facilitating agencies play a critical role in the advertising industry. These agencies provide various specialized services and expertise to help advertisers plan, create, execute, and optimize their advertising campaigns.All advertisers, by definition, use some form of media to accomplish organizational objectives. Where significant amounts of media expenditures are involved, the advertiser will also use the services of an advertising agency and one or more research suppliers. Together, these three types of institutions make up the primary facilitating institutions of advertising management. These facilitating institutions in advertising, including advertisers, advertising agencies, and research suppliers, play vital roles in achieving organizational objectives.

FACILITATING AGENCIES

Facilitating agencies play a critical role in the advertising industry. These agencies provide various specialized services and expertise to help advertisers plan, create, execute, and optimize their advertising campaigns. The specific services offered by facilitating agencies can vary, but they typically fall into several categories:

1. **Advertising Agencies:** Advertising agencies are among the most well-known facilitating agencies in the industry. They provide a range of services, including market research, campaign planning and strategy, creative development (such as ad

copywriting and design), media planning and buying, and campaign tracking and analysis. Advertising agencies often work with clients to develop comprehensive advertising campaigns that span multiple media channels.

2. **Media Buying Agencies:** Media buying agencies specialize in negotiating and purchasing advertising space or time across various media channels, such as television, radio, print, online, and out-of-home advertising. They help advertisers secure the most cost-effective and strategic placements for their ads.

3. **Public Relations (PR) Agencies:** PR agencies focus on managing a company's public image and reputation. They help create and distribute press releases, organize events, manage media relations, and respond to crises, all with the goal of positively shaping public perception.

4. **Digital Marketing Agencies:** Digital marketing agencies are experts in online advertising and marketing. They provide services such as search engine optimization (SEO), search engine marketing (SEM), social media marketing, email marketing, content creation, and website design and development.

5. **Creative Agencies:** Creative agencies specialize in developing compelling and visually engaging content for advertising campaigns. They may create ad designs, videos, animations, and other creative assets that resonate with the target audience.

6. **Market Research Agencies:** Market research agencies conduct consumer and market research to gather valuable insights that inform advertising strategies. This includes surveys, focus groups, and data analysis to understand consumer behaviour and preferences.

7. **Production Houses:** Production houses are responsible for producing audiovisual content, including TV commercials, radio ads, online videos, and other multimedia elements. They handle everything from scriptwriting to filming and editing.

8. **Event Management Agencies:** Event management agencies focus on planning and executing marketing events, product launches, and promotional campaigns. They create memorable experiences for consumers to engage with brands.

9. **Media Monitoring and Analytics Agencies:** These agencies provide tools and services to track and analyze the performance of advertising campaigns. They help advertisers measure the impact of their advertising efforts and make data-driven decisions for optimization.

10. **AdTech and MarTech Companies:** These technology companies offer advertising and marketing software solutions, including programmatic advertising platforms, customer relationship management (CRM) tools, and data analytics platforms that enable advertisers to streamline their campaigns and gather insights.

11. **Creative Production Companies:** These companies specialize in producing high-quality content, such as videos, animations, and graphics, for advertising campaigns. They work closely with advertisers to bring their creative vision to life.

    Collaborating with facilitating agencies allows advertisers to tap into specialized expertise and resources, leading to more effective and efficient advertising campaigns. The choice of which agencies to work with depends on an advertiser's specific goals, target audience, budget, and the nature of the campaign.

ADVERTISING AGENCY

An advertising agency is a company that aids its clients in creating advertisements and other commercially viable content to sell a brand, a product, or a company. An agency's professionals can meet with their clients to ascertain their advertising requirements. From there, they can create plans in accordance with the client's directives or work together on the client's advertising plans. Some advertising firms provide clients with a whole service, which encompasses everything a client would need, or they can concentrate on a particular speciality, like social media.

ROLE OF ADVERTISING AGENCY

An advertising agency is a specialized firm or company that provides a wide range of services related to the planning, creation, execution, and management of advertising and marketing campaigns on behalf of clients, typically businesses and organizations. Following functions are being performed by an advertising agency:

1. **Market Research and Analysis:** Advertising agencies conduct market research to understand the target audience, market trends, and competition. This data informs campaign strategy and creative development.
2. **Campaign Planning and Strategy:** Agencies work with clients to define advertising objectives and develop a comprehensive advertising strategy. This includes setting goals, selecting target demographics, and determining the best channels and messages to reach the audience effectively.
3. **Creative Development:** Advertising agencies are responsible for creating compelling and engaging ad content. This includes copywriting for advertisements, designing visual elements, and often creating multimedia content like videos or graphics.
4. **Media Planning and Buying:** Agencies have expertise in media planning and purchasing advertising space or time. They negotiate with various media outlets to secure the best placements and deals for their clients. This can include television, radio, print, online, and out-of-home advertising.

5. **Campaign Execution:** Agencies manage the actual execution of the advertising campaign. This involves coordinating creative assets, scheduling ad placements, and ensuring that the campaign runs smoothly.

6. **Ad Placement and Tracking:** Agencies monitor the performance of advertisements to ensure they are meeting the campaign's objectives. They may use analytics tools and tracking systems to measure metrics like click-through rates, conversion rates, and return on investment (ROI).

7. **Optimization:** Based on campaign performance, agencies make adjustments to optimize results. This can include tweaking ad copy, visuals, or media placements to improve effectiveness.

8. **Brand Management:** Advertising agencies help clients manage their brand image and reputation through consistent messaging and creative content.

9. **Strategic Consulting:** Agencies provide strategic guidance to clients on marketing and advertising-related decisions. They may advise on product launches, market positioning, and competitive analysis.

10. **Campaign Evaluation and Reporting:** At the end of a campaign, agencies analyze the results and prepare comprehensive reports for clients. These reports help clients understand the impact of their advertising efforts.

11. **Creative Services:** Some agencies specialize in creative services, such as graphic design, video production, and content creation, and may offer these services independently or as part of a broader advertising campaign.

12. **Digital Marketing:** Many modern advertising agencies specialize in digital marketing, including search engine optimization (SEO), search engine marketing (SEM), social media marketing, email marketing, and website development.

    Advertising agencies bring a combination of creative talent, marketing expertise, and industry knowledge to help clients effectively promote their products or services. They aim to create and execute advertising campaigns that resonate with the target audience, enhance brand visibility, and ultimately drive desired outcomes, such as increased sales or brand recognition. The level of involvement and the specific services an agency provides can vary depending on the client's needs and objectives.

TYPES OF ADVERTISING AGENCY

1. Full-service advertising agencies :

Full-service advertising agencies offer a wide variety of advertising services to its clients, with both traditional and digital options. Clients may choose this type of agency when they desire several advertising options for their brand. Advertisers may choose to work at this agency if they're skilled in an assortment of advertisement skills and enjoy switching between tasks for campaigns. For example, in one campaign, a professional may work on the traditional advertisement and in another campaign, the professional may work on the digital deliverables. Some options a full-service advertising agency are television advertisements, advertisement campaigns, content creation, search engine optimization (SEO), social media management, radio advertisements, web development etc.

2. Digital advertising agencies

Digital advertising agencies offer advertising services online. Clients may choose this agency when they only desire to have digital advertisements rather than tangible advertising goods. Professionals may choose to work at this agency when they're passionate about digital advertisement and their strengths are in this area. Other professionals, other than advertisers, can work in this agency, including copywriters, videographers and photographers. Digital advertising agencies offer email marketing, social media marketing, website design and marketing, lead generation etc.

3. Traditional advertising agencies

Traditional advertising agencies offer classic styles of advertising for clients. Clients may choose this agency when they're advertising their business to the local area. Professionals may choose to work at this agency if they have a passion for implementing traditional advertising strategies into campaigns for clients. They offer services like billboard advertisements, television commercial advertisements, newspaper advertisements, radio advertisements, magazine advertisements etc.

4. Social media advertising agencies

Social media advertising agencies offer its clients social media-focused advertising. Companies or brands may choose to have this agency help them with their advertising if they desire an increase in their social media engagement or more traffic going to their website through their social media accounts. Professionals work with their clients to ensure the advertising strategy aligns with their business strategies. Some services offered are establishing social media advertisement optimization, design profiles, write blog posts, produce videos, create content, write captions etc.

5. Creative boutiques

Creative boutiques offer a variety of creative design options for its clients based on their needs. This type of agency allows clients to monitor how their campaign is performing on their own. A creative boutique also allows clients the ability to choose where they place their advertisements. For example, they can choose to place them as an online banner on third-party websites or as sponsored social media posts. A client may choose this agency when they lack creative professionals to produce the desired content.Professionals may choose to work at a creative boutique because they can create the content and give the analytical portion to the client.

6. Media buying agencies

Media buying agencies work with their clients to choose the best location to place their advertising material. This can include deciding where most consumers may view the material and who is more likely to act on the advertisement when they see it. In this agency, it can include both digital and print campaigns. For example, if a client has a television advertisement for their small pizza shop business, a professional at this agency may suggest placing the television advertisement on a local channel during the news slot.

7. Public relations advertising agencies

Public relations (PR) advertising agencies help their clients enhance and maintain their public image. The public image can include the company, its employees and the CEO. A PR advertisement agency can work with companies to feature their business in the news, local or digital community and other industry websites. Clients may choose to use a PR advertising agency to improve the public image of their brand or increase public awareness about them. Professionals may choose to work at this agency because they're passionate about public relations and collaborating with brands.

8. Brand advertising agencies

Brand advertising agencies offer a specialty in branding for clients. Branding is a company's name, logo, colours and overall design that differentiates them from other companies. The goal of branding is to make it recognizable and memorable for consumers to recall. Professionals working at these agencies conduct brand and industry research to determine an effective plan for a brand. Clients may choose this agency when they're starting a new business or wanting a rebranding of their existing business. Some services a brand advertising agency may offer include logo designs, signage, brand name development etc.

9. In-house advertising agencies

In-house advertising agencies are agencies that operate within an existing company. This means the agency exists to operate for a single client, which is the company that owns them. For example, a multi-national clothing company has created its own advertising agency in the office to focus on creating an advertising campaign for the clothing company. Clients may choose this because it saves them money from outsourcing the work. It can also make communication easier when the agency exists where the company is operating.

10. Interactive advertising agencies

Interactive advertising agencies are like digital advertising agencies, but it focuses on the consumer interacting with the advertisement online. For example, a client may request to send their advertisement to mobile phones as personal messages if the consumer opts into the messages. This is interactive to the consumer because it comes to their phone, often with a link they can click on and follow to the website. Clients may choose this advertiser to increase their online engagement and encourage consumers to click on the advertisements that redirect them to their site.

IMPORTANT QUESTIONS

1. What are facilitating agencies and what role they play in the growth of a business?
2. Explain the different types of facilitating agencies?
3. What is an advertising agency and how it helps the companies to flourish their business?
4. Explain different types of advertising agencies that can assist brands to market their products and services.

❍❍❍

Chapter 9

ATTENTION AND COMPREHENSION

INTRODUCTION

Attention is like a spotlight for your brain. It helps you focus on certain things and ignore the rest. When something grabs your attention, like a loud noise or a bright light, it sends a message to your brain. Your brain decides if it's important or not.Imagine you're in a huge supermarket with lots of stuff on the shelves. There's no way you can look at every single item, it would take forever! So, you have to pick what you want to look at, like your favorite snacks or groceries.The same goes for TV and radio. They show a ton of ads, but you can't pay attention to all of them. You choose to listen to the ones that interest you and ignore the rest.In a world with so much information, you have to be picky about what you pay attention to.The average supermarket has 30,000 individual items. It would take hours to attend each of them. Each television network shows 6000 commercial ads per week and radio stations air many more. Therefore, consumers must be selective in attending to marketing as well as other messages.

ATTENTION AND COMPREHENSION

Attention is a state of sensory clearness with a margin and a focus. Attention is the aspect of consciousness that relates to the amount of effort exerted in focusing on certain aspects of an experience, so that they become relatively vivid.

With so much stuff competing for our attention, like ads on TV that we can skip with our remote controls, it's getting really hard for ads to grab our attention. And because people are switching channels and avoiding ads, even when ads do get seen, they don't really get the message across as well as they should. Studies have found that ads are only fully or partly understood about 20 to 30 percent of the time.

So, whether an ad wants to make us remember it, change our thoughts about a brand, or make us buy something, there are two important things that need to happen. First, we have to see the ad and pay attention to it. Then, when we do pay attention, we need to understand it the way the advertiser wanted us to. If we misunderstand it, the ad won't work the way it's supposed to.

Think of attention like a filter for information. It decides what we notice and what we ignore. But it's not easy to get our attention because we often try to avoid things we don't want to see or hear. There are so many ads everywhere, like in magazines, and it's hard for one ad to stand out and be remembered. Ads also have a tough time when there are lots of other ads for similar products.

COMBATING CLUTTER, ZAPPING AND ZIPPING

Clutter

One big problem for advertisers today is that it's really hard to get people's attention because there are so many ads everywhere. But not all ads are affected the same way by this problem. Some research found that ads placed at the very beginning or the very end of a bunch of ads on TV are less affected by this issue than ads in the middle. So, it's a good idea for advertisers to try to get their ads in those prime spots. In the print medium, several advertisers have tried to fight clutter by using devices as varied as three-dimensional pop-ups to musical microchips in their magazine ads. These ads can cost millions of dollars apiece, but they do succeed in getting nearly 100 percent leadership.

Zapping

Now, let's talk about "zapping." A little while ago, TV advertisers were worried that people might leave the room during commercial breaks. But now, there's a bigger problem—people can skip the commercials without leaving their seats. Viewers can mute the sound, change channels with their remote control, or fast-forward through ads when they're watching a recorded show. Homes with remote controls for their TVs skip ads 60 percent more than homes without remotes. And more and more homes have these remotes.

The best way to fight zapping (and zipping, which is fast-forwarding through ads) is to make ads that are so interesting that people want to watch them instead of skipping them. Research shows that people tend to skip ads the most during the first five seconds, so it's really important to grab their attention right away. Advertisers can do this by offering useful information, making ads that are cool and exciting, and making ads that match what people already think and feel. For most people, the interesting and new parts of an ad are more important than the useful information, especially if they're not super interested in the product.In making such ads, the "interesting" and "novel" elements appear to be more important than the "useful information" aspects, at least for casual, low-involvement viewers.

Zipping

A study found that consumers playing back prerecorded programs on their video cassette recorders tend to zip through ads over 60 percent of the time. Another study looking at consumers zipping through videotaped programs and ads also found that while most consumers zipping through ads whipped through all ads indiscriminately, trying to avoid all of them, zipping rates were lowest for the first commercial in the first slot and highest for the commercials in the last slot. So, while it appears far more difficult to fight zipping than zapping, early slot placement might offer some hope. Other advertisers combat zipping by developing commercials that use visual elements(such as brand logos or package shots) that will be visible even if the viewer is fast-forwarding through the ad. Brand dominance strategy does appear to inhibit the reducing effects of zipping on attitude toward the ad, brand beliefs, and purchase intentions.

CREATING ADS THAT ATTRACT ATTENTION

The filter that controls our attention works in different ways, depending on how much effort and awareness we put into it. On one end, there's active searching, where someone actively looks for information. They might ask their friends for opinions or read magazines they don't usually read to find what they need.Moving along, there's passive searching. In this case, a person only looks for information from sources they come across in their everyday life.Lastly, there's passive attention. Here, someone doesn't really need the information right away, and they don't actively try to get it. But sometimes, information can still come into their awareness without them trying.

In all three situations, it's important to understand why someone seeks information so that advertisements can be created to grab their attention effectively. There are numerous reasons for seeking information, which vary depending on the circumstances and the individual. Nevertheless, it's helpful to explore four general motivations for paying attention to informative messages.The first motivation is to acquire information that can be very useful to a person. In the context of advertising, individuals seek product information that can help them make better choices when buying things.Secondly, people might want to come across information that supports their existing beliefs and avoid information that contradicts their views.Thirdly, there's a desire to encounter information that excites or arouses interest.Lastly, individuals are motivated to find things that captivate their attention because they find them intriguing. These motivations will be discussed one by one.

1. Information of Practical Value

It may appear a bit repetitive to state that advertising actually provides information, and people indeed rely on this information when making choices. Even though advertising experts and researchers often seek subtle and concealed reasons for why certain ads are more memorable than others, it's important not to underestimate the straightforward and main purpose of advertising, which is to inform. In fact, psychologists point to studies that prove people seek out information that is useful to them in their daily lives. At this point, it should be evident to the reader that such evidence is not necessary. Clearly, there is a real demand for product information, and effective advertisements typically meet this demand.

Numerous advertising copywriters have observed that, based on their experience, many advertisements that excel in capturing attention (as seen in factors like coupon redemption) often feature headlines that pledge valuable, cost-free information. One particularly effective headline format, for example, is to use "How to..." in the context of the problem the consumer is trying to solve with the purchase of a specific product. Consider a consumer looking to buy a refrigerator; they are highly likely to take notice of and engage with an advertisement that, right in its headline, provides guidance on "How to choose the perfect refrigerator for your requirements."

A general theory of motivation that the behavioral tendency to process information is based upon three factors.

- The first is the need for information about some topic. Obviously, audience members will have more information need for some products than others. For example, products that are costly, complex, or somewhat unknown because they are new or for some other reason will have associated with them an information need.
- The second is the expectancy (probability) that processing a particular ad will lead to relevant information exposure.
- The third would be a measure of the value of that particular as a source of relevant information: the goodness or badness of the message as an information source. This structure provides an approach to determine the extent to which a person might be motivated to process information from a particular

(a) Long Copy

An advertisement with concise text can still convey information effectively. When introducing a new brand or model in a familiar product category with distinct and noteworthy features, it might not need any text at all. Nevertheless, in numerous scenarios, a genuinely informative advertisement benefits from having a more extensive body of text. Unfortunately, the widespread belief in the advertising industry discourages the use of longer text, resulting in advertising content that lacks depth. This belief asserts that advertising copy must be brief and attention-grabbing to be read, assuming that readers will shy away from lengthy and daunting content.

While this rule may hold true for certain products and situations, it certainly doesn't apply universally. If a reader genuinely finds the information valuable and it's presented effectively, they can be encouraged to read a longer piece of content. Moreover, it's often not a significant loss if some readers who don't need the information decide not to read it because they aren't motivated to do so.The ideal length of your content depends on the product you're advertising. For instance, if you're promoting chewing gum, there's not much to say, so keep your content brief. However, if you're advertising a product with numerous compelling qualities, it makes sense to use longer content because the more you explain, the more likely you are to persuade potential buyers.

(b) Infomercials

One method advertisers employ to convey extensive information to TV viewers is through the use of infomercials. These are lengthy programs, typically lasting around thirty minutes, that delve deeply into the product's features. Many well-known advertisers, including Apple and Kodak (for their photo-CD product), have adopted the use of infomercials. In the past, infomercials were primarily associated with less reputable direct response campaigns advertising low-quality goods on late-night television shows. However, as infomercials have gained greater credibility and acceptance, even established marketing clients have started using them. In fact, some major advertising agency networks have either acquired or established divisions dedicated to producing infomercials.

(c) Active Search

There are situations where consumers won't find enough information from their usual sources to make informed decisions. In such cases, they may proactively seek information from advertising in specialized magazines, ask for opinions from others, or read technical reports.This active search for information is highly significant because the information is very relevant to the consumer. Such encounters are more likely to influence what the consumer knows about a product and how they feel about it compared to information received passively. Additionally, when actively seeking information, the consumer is often closer to making a purchase, so they are less likely to forget the message. Active search tends to happen more when there is a lot of risk and uncertainty involved, such as when making significant purchases, choosing products that require more consideration, or when dealing with new products. The need for information is highest when dealing with entirely new products and lowest when consumers are very familiar with a brand. As consumers become loyal to a specific brand, their need for information about that product decreases. For instance, people who consistently buy the same car brand are less likely to shop around compared to those who switch to a different brand.

(d) Future Reference

A person doesn't have to plan an immediate purchase to gather information about a product. It makes sense to gather such information for future reference, using methods like passive search or passive attention that we've explained earlier. Actively searching for information can take time and effort, but these costs can be avoided or minimized if someone stays updated about a particular type of product. For instance, young adults might stay informed about smart watches in anticipation of a future purchase. Of course, there may be other reasons motivating them as well.

2. Information that Supports

A natural and intuitively appealing hypothesis is that people have a psychological preference for supportive information. It follows that they therefore tend to avoid non-supportive or discrepant information.

(a) Selective Exposure

Selective exposure can be understood through consistency theories like dissonance theory, which propose that people naturally strive to maintain consistent thoughts and actions regarding things. According to dissonance theory, having conflicting thoughts (cognitive dissonance) creates discomfort, and people will seek to alleviate this discomfort. One way to do this is through selective exposure, which involves seeking information that aligns with their existing beliefs and avoiding information that contradicts them.

(b) Involuntary Exposure

Selective exposure tends to increase when an individual's standpoint is challenged by being exposed to information that doesn't support their views involuntarily. For instance, consider someone who has a strong and loyal preference for one or more car models. Now, let's say they hear a rumor about a government report suggesting that one of their favored models might have a feature leading to transmission problems. In this situation, the person might become more attentive to information that backs up their existing belief, like the model's reliability.In response, an advertiser could prepare to promptly address any negative information their customers might come across. Such a campaign would take advantage of this selectiveness and could be quite effective. Its primary audience would be existing customers, including loyal ones, rather than those who aren't currently buying the brand.

(c) Combating Selective Exposure

What methods can advertisers employ to tackle selective exposure, whether it's obvious or more subtle? One strategy involves providing incentives such as rewards, contests, or exclusive gifts to motivate individuals to interact with the content. In the context of direct-mail advertising, leveraging contests has demonstrated remarkable effectiveness in overcoming the selective-exposure challenge. Alternatively, another approach is to avoid directly pinpointing particular audience segments and instead utilize an indirect two-step process. This method entails initially reaching out to influential opinion leaders and subsequently relying on word-of-mouth to extend the message to a wider audience.

3. Information that Stimulates

There are some theories called complexity theories. They don't always give predictions that are the same, like other theories do. People naturally like things that are new, surprising, different, and complicated because these things make them happy. When we talk about new and surprising things, we mean the difference between what we already know and what we might know in the future. So, trying out new things can sometimes make our ideas inconsistent.

This theory is based on the idea that people get bored over time, and they want to get rid of that boredom by finding new, unusual, and unique things to do. People are naturally curious about the world around them, and this curiosity makes them want to find information that challenges what they already know or believe in.

Apple's application of complex theories in its marketing strategy has been highly successful. By offering a variety of innovative features, introducing changes in product design, and presenting intricate technical details, Apple keeps consumers engaged and curious about their products. This approach not only maintains a dedicated customer base but also attracts new customers who are intrigued by the uniqueness and complexity of Apple's offerings.In this way, Apple's marketing strategy is a prime example of how complexity theories can be effectively used in the real world to create interest, engagement, and loyalty among consumers.

4. Ad Characteristics

Several factors contribute to an advertisement's ability to grab people's attention. The size and brightness of an ad often play a significant role in capturing attention. When it comes to ad size, larger advertisements tend to attract more attention, although the relationship isn't necessarily linear. Research has shown that full-page ads in four colors score about 85 percent higher in readership than half-page ads in four colors.Advertisements that are visually "loud" or more intense are more likely to be noticed compared to those with lower intensity. Additionally, presentations in color generally garner more attention than black and white ads. The use of four colors can lead to approximately 50 percent more readership than black and white for both one-page and two-page ads.The placement of an ad can also impact its visibility. Ads positioned on the left side of a page and in the upper half tend to receive slightly more readership due to people's reading habits. Moreover, research suggests that ads placed at the back of a magazine can attract roughly 65 percent more readers than those positioned in the middle. Ads featured on the inside covers (front and back) tend to capture approximately 30 percent more readers.

Research has also emphasized the attention-grabbing qualities of "vivid" information, which refers to information that is tangible rather than theoretical, evokes mental images, stirs emotions, and includes extensive details and specifics about objects, actions, outcomes, and the context in which they occur. Some have proposed that advertising expressed in clear, detailed, and specific terms will capture more attention (and have a greater influence on shaping judgments about product quality) compared to content phrased in vague and general terms.However, it's important to note that the message itself needs to possess vividness, not just its presentation. Moreover, consumers should process the information by creating mental images related to it. Vivid but unrelated information may initially grab attention but might not be mentally processed and, as a result, may have no impact on subsequent attitudes.

(a) Forestalling Ad Wearout via Pool-Outs

It's pretty clear that in advertising, being too predictable isn't a good idea, especially when people can easily ignore ads. Let's talk about a special case where an advertiser keeps showing the same ad to the same group of people many times. When people see the exact same ad over and over, they stop paying attention to it. This is called the "ad wear-out" problem.To avoid this problem, it's a good idea to show slightly different versions of the same ad, using what we call "pool-outs." Researchers have found that when you use these variations, people pay more attention compared to showing the same ad all the time. But here's the interesting part: if these variations are different enough from each other, they can create many different thoughts about the brand in the viewer's mind. This makes it easier for people to remember the brand name later, leading to better brand recall.

So, in simple terms, it's best not to show the same ad too many times because people will get bored. Instead, make small changes to the ad and show those variations. When these variations are quite different from each other, people remember the brand name better.

5. Information that Interests

People tend to pay attention to things that they find interesting. And what they find interesting is usually connected to things they are personally involved with or care about. Basically, people are most interested in themselves, and things related to them.You can see this connection between interest and attention when you look at how many people read different types of advertisements. For example, men are much more likely to read ads for cars compared to ads for women's clothes, toiletries, insurance, or building materials. On the other hand, women are most interested in ads for movies and women's clothing, and they pay less attention to ads for travel, men's clothing, liquor, or machinery.

One of the best ways to make sure people pay attention to an ad is by making it all about them. This means mentioning their name and talking about what they do. However, this is usually only possible in direct marketing, like personalized letters.Another way to get attention is by talking about things that are important to the people you're trying to reach. For example, if there's a big topic everyone cares about, like taking care of the environment and recycling, you can tie your ad to that topic. If you do it right, people will likely have a positive view of your ad because it's connected to something they care about.

For example: Nike

Nike can capture people's attention in two ways:

- **Personalized Approach:** They can send personalized emails to customers, addressing them by name and recommending products based on their past purchases. This makes customers feel recognized and valued.
- **Topical Approach:** Nike can create ads focused on important social or environmental issues, like sustainability. This aligns their brand with relevant topics and appeals to customers who care about these issues, capturing their attention and enhancing their brand image.

RECALL

Recall is typically a more important ad objective in low involvement situations, because consumers may not go through a great degree of thinking about which brand to buy. In high-involvement situations, consumers typically use more brand-attribute information in deciding which brand is better for them, so persuasion becomes very important—but recall of the brand, and the attributes of the brand, is obviously still necessary, because the actual brand choice will likely occur at some point in time after the ad was seen. In both kinds of situations, therefore, an ad has not only to attract attention, but also to communicate the brand name and the brand benefits in a memorable way.

How can ads make sure people remember the brand and its message better?There are several ways to do this:

- **Show the Ad More Often:** One way is to show the ad more times. You can do this by having a bigger budget for advertising or by showing the ad to the same people more times. You might also use shorter ads on TV or cheaper advertising methods like radio or outdoor ads.
- **Make the Ad Different and Special:** Another way is to make the ad really unique and interesting. Ads that stand out and are different from others are not only more likely to get noticed but also remembered.
- **Repeat Important Stuff:** In the ad itself, say the brand name and the main message more than once. Some ads on TV and radio repeat these things three times or even more in a single commercial.
- **Catchy Phrases or Songs:** Lastly, you can use catchy slogans or songs in the ad. These help people remember the brand and what makes it special, long after they've seen the ad.

ATTENTION VS. COMPREHENSION

The ways we've talked about to make an ad more attention-grabbing can be thought of as using interesting things in the ad to get people's attention. The goal is to make the entire ad more noticeable. However, advertisers need to be careful not to grab attention in a way that distracts from the main message.For example, using very attractive models can get a lot of people's attention, but it can also take their focus away from the main message about the brand. Sometimes, ads that are too explicit or sexy can make people think more about how the ad looks rather than what the brand is saying. So, while people might remember the ad and the brand name, they might forget the important details about the brand itself.

These trade-offs don't just happen with the use of sex in advertising; they can happen with other things like humor, celebrities, and more. What this means is that sometimes, a part of an ad can become the center of attention, but if that part isn't related to what the ad is supposed to achieve, it can actually harm the ad's effectiveness.So, for advertisers, it's not enough to just create ads that grab attention, even though that's important. They also need to make sure that the important messages in the ad get across. Understanding what the ad is trying to say, especially why the brand is better, is crucial for making people believe in and like the brand.To put it simply, if people don't get the main points in an ad about why a brand is better, they might focus on less important things like who's in the ad. But if they do understand, they are more likely to form opinions about the brand based on the important reasons, rather than just who's endorsing it.

COMPREHENSION VS. INTERPRETATION

Basis	Comprehension	Interpretation
DEFINITION	Comprehension refers to the ability of a person to understand the basic message and information conveyed in an advertisement.	Interpretation refers to the process of extracting deeper meaning, emotions, and associations from an advertisement beyond the literal message.
PROCESS	It involves processing the language, visuals, and other elements of the advertisement to extract the literal meaning.	It involves analyzing the symbolism, tone, imagery, and subtext of the advertisement to derive a broader understanding of its intended impact and the emotions it aims to evoke.
GOALS	The primary goal of comprehension in advertising is to ensure that the audience grasps the fundamental message, product features, benefits, and any other essential information being presented.	The goal of interpretation in advertising is to create a more profound and lasting impression on the audience. It allows advertisers to connect with viewers on an emotional or psychological level and often leads to a more memorable and persuasive ad.

Suppose you see a car advertisement. Comprehension would involve understanding the basic information such as the car's make and model, its price, and its key features. Interpretation, on the other hand, might involve looking beyond the basics and understanding that the advertisement is trying to convey a sense of luxury, adventure, or status. It might evoke feelings of aspiration or desire, and you might associate the car with freedom and success.

In summary, while comprehension focuses on understanding the surface-level content of an advertisement, interpretation delves deeper into the emotional and symbolic aspects, aiming to create a more profound and lasting impression on the audience. Both are important in advertising, as effective advertisements often balance both comprehension and interpretation to engage and persuade their target audience.

IMPORTANT QUESTIONS

1. What do you understand by attention? How can consumers attention be grabbed by the marketers?
2. What is the difference between attention and comprehension?
3. How can ads be frames to attract customers attention?
4. How marketers can increase consumer recall?
5. What is the difference between zipping, zapping and clutter? How can they be reduced?

❍❍❍

Chapter 10

Understanding Benefit-Based Attitude

INTRODUCTION

The manager needs to figure out what the message should talk about. It could be about the good things the product does (if so, which ones), building a certain image for the brand (if so, what kind of image), making people feel a certain way about the brand, or making the brand look cool by making it popular among a group. This chapter is all about deciding which good things to talk about to change what people think about the brand. Usually, ads want to highlight the good stuff and focus on the things that make the product look better. Sometimes, it's also okay to talk about the not-so-good things about the brand. The important thing is to know what matters when people choose a brand and what's most important in the specific market where the product is sold. And, to see if a certain advertising strategy will really work, we need to know if the product's qualities and the way it's seen are connected to what people think about it.

ATTITUDE LEVELS AND COMPONENTS

Attitude is a central concept in the entire field of social psychology, and theories and methods associated with its explanation and measurement have largely evolved from the work of social psychologists and psychometricians.The most widely held view of the structure of an attitude is that it is made up of three closely interrelated, components:

- cognitive (awareness, comprehension, knowledge),
- affective (evaluation, likin preference), and
- conative (action tendencies such as intentions, trial, or purchase).

Usually, people pay the most attention to how they feel about something when they decide if they like it. It's thought that this liking comes from what we think about the thing (like the good things we know about the brand) and then makes us want to try it or not. In simple terms, we buy things because we like them, and we like them because we think they're good for us.But some people say that we can like things without really thinking about why they're good. They think our emotions can make us like something, even if we don't think about the benefits. For now, let's imagine we're in a situation where people do think about what's good about different brands before they decide if they like them. In these cases, we need to know how to figure out if people like the brand overall and what they think about it. This helps us create ads that make peopie like our brand more.

MEASUREMENT OF ATTITUDE

Measuring attitude is like finding out if someone likes or dislikes a brand. We can ask people directly if they like it or not, or we can ask them to rate how much they like it on a scale from very good to very bad. This is useful to know if people like a brand, but it doesn't tell us why.To understand why someone likes or dislikes a brand, we use models that assume this overall liking comes from thinking about what's good or bad about the brand. We ask people to rate the brand on different aspects or features. For example, we might ask them to say if the brand is good or bad in terms of several qualities. Then, we take the average of their scores to measure their attitude. These measurements are called "multiattribute evaluations" because they're based on looking at the different qualities that make up the overall attitude toward the brand.

1. Direct Measures of Overall Attitude

The easiest way to find out what someone thinks about something, like a brand or a product, is to simply ask if they like it or not. They don't have to explain why, just a simple "yes" or "no." If we want to know how much they like it, we can use a scale. For example, we can ask them to rate how much they like it on a scale from "really like it a lot" (1) to "don't like it at all" (7). We can also use other words like "excellent to poor" or "good to bad" to ask the same question.

A big question is whether our opinions about a brand affect our choices and actions in the market. Of course, we need to measure these opinions in a way that's closely connected to the actions we're trying to predict. But, even if we measure these opinions accurately, it doesn't always mean that liking a brand will lead to buying it. For example, someone might really like a brand, but they might not be able to afford it or have a reason to buy it. Many teenagers might really like Porsches, but very few of them can actually buy one.Also, what's happening in the moment when they decide to buy something or if they make a sudden choice can change what we expected based on their attitude that was measured earlier. Lastly, people might buy a brand even if they don't really like it, because they think experts or their friends like it, suggest it, or will be impressed by it.Information about a brand obtained through advertising is relatively less "direct." Repeated advertising exposure, however, can increase how much information the consumer has about the brand, which canincrease the confidence with which attitudes are held and thus increase their impact on behavior.

2. Importance of the Attributes that Cause Overall Attitude

In the competitive world, it's often challenging to grab a consumer's attention and convey multiple ideas. That's why it's crucial to figure out which attributes matter the most when people make decisions. For instance, when a toothpaste company wants to promote its product, should they focus on preventing cavities, making teeth whiter, ensuring fresh breath, or highlighting the taste? Similarly, when a university wants to attract students, should they emphasize the reputation of their professors, the campus environment, or special aspects of their teaching and research programs?

These questions are all about finding out which qualities are most important when it comes to forming and changing attitudes, which ultimately affects what people decide to buy. Every product, service, or choice has a set of qualities that play a role in decision-making. For example, when choosing between Coke and Pepsi, taste is a critical attribute.

Attributes can be examined at different levels. There's a difference between physical qualities (like color, sweetness, or weight), pseudo-physical qualities (like spiciness or fragrance), and benefits (things that make consumers' lives better). These attributes can be used to position and select products or services. Psychological benefits often fall into the category of benefits or pseudo-physical qualities.

3. Means Ends and Laddering Analysis

Another useful way of distinguishing between the different levels of attributes is through the means-end chain model." This model focuses on the connection be-tween product attributes, consumer consequences, and personal values, through a process called "laddering":

product attributes → consumer consequences → personal values

In this model, values are like the things people want in life. They can be about how you feel in the outside world, like feeling important or accepted. Or, they can be about how you see yourself, like having self-esteem, happiness, security, being neat, or feeling accom-plished.Product attributes and consumer consequences are the ways to get those things you want. Product attributes are the things you can measure about a product, like how fast a car can go or how quickly food cooks. They can also be the things you can't measure, like how good something tastes, its strong flavor, or how stylish it looks. Consumer consequences are the results you get from using a product. They can be practical, like saving money or not needing to wash your hair every day. Or they can be about how you see yourself, like making more friends, having fun, or feeling more attractive.

The idea here is that to create effective ads, we need to understand the connections between these attributes, consequences, and values. It's not enough to just talk about the product's features. Advertisements should also highlight the good things that come from using the product and show how it can help people achieve what they value in life.

4. Identifying Important Attributes or Benefits

There are many ways to figure out and rank the importance of the qualities that people use to judge and compare brands. Sometimes, we already know these qualities from past experience or research. In other cases, we have to do new research to find out what these qualities are.Once we know these qualities, we need to understand which ones matter the most. Advertisers want to know how important each quality is. We can use different tools like surveys where people rate or rank the qualities. There are also more advanced methods like conjoint analysis, which asks people to consider different levels of each quality. The next sections will show examples of these methods.

(a) Rating, Ranking and Conjoint Analysis

We can study the important qualities or advantages, instead of focusing on specific brands or things. We use methods like the ones we used to measure overall attitude to figure out how important these qualities are. One simple way is to ask people to put a list of qualities in order from most important to least important, like voting in an election. The qualities that get the most "votes" are the ones that matter the most.

Rating method:A simple way to rate these qualities is to list them and have a scale from "very important" to "very unimportant" next to each. People just need to mark how important each quality is when they're deciding what to buy.Another way is to use something called a "Likert scale." Instead of just a scale, we use statements like "It would be very important for me to know if the next tire I buy is steel-belted or nylon-belted." Then, people say how much they agree or disagree with each statement to show how important they think that quality is.

Rating rating: Direct rating and ranking methods are cost-effective and simple to use. The idea is, if some qualities are not so important, this will be clear when we look at the data. However, there's a challenge. People often want everything and rate everything as important. Most products involve a balance of good qualities, and the direct methods don't always show this balance.What advertisers really want to know is how much people are willing to give up one good thing for another. For instance, if you're choosing a phone, are you ready to trade a bigger screen for a longer battery life, or vice versa? The direct methods might not tell us this, but its what advertisers want to understand.

Conjoint analysis: Direct methods have another issue. They don't tell us how much of a quality you really want. They just give you the quality without different levels of it.To fix this, there's a method called conjoint analysis. Instead of just looking at single qualities, this method asks people to make choices between different combinations of quality levels. It helps us understand how important each quality level is. Conjoint analysis is similar to ranking and rating methods, but it works a bit differently in how we collect and study the data.Conjoint analysis is a valuable tool for product development and marketing because it helps businesses design products and services that better match what customers want.For example, if a company wants to understand what kind of smartphone people prefer, they might create different smartphone options with variations in features like screen size, camera quality, and battery life. People would then choose their favorite option, and the company could use this information to design a smartphone that's more likely to be popular.

(b) Leverage and Determinant Attributes

An attribute with high leverage has a big influence on your overall opinion. This influence comes from how important that attribute is and how it affects other attributes in your thinking. Sometimes, an attribute can indirectly affect other attributes. For example, the style of a car might be important because it not only matters by itself but also affects how you see its performance and convenience. So, if you change your perception of a brand's style, it might impact how you feel about its performance and convenience more than you'd expect.

There are different ways to measure this influence. One way is to see how strongly one attribute is linked to others in your mind. If an attribute is not connected to others, it might not have much extra influence beyond its importance. But if it's closely tied to other attributes, it can have more influence than its importance alone suggests.Another approach is to deliberately change how you see a brand on a particular feature and see how it affects your overall opinion. The attributes that have the biggest impact on your overall opinion are the ones with high leverage.

5. USING MULTI-ATTRIBUTE ATTITUDE MODELS

There are dozens of models and theories about the connection between perception and preference or attributes and attitudes." In this section, the basic principles underlying each of these model classes are presented and assessed, and examples are given of their application to advertising.

(a) Evaluative Belief Models of Cognitive Structure

A cognitive structure model assumes that a person forms an attitude toward an object by developing beliefs about that object and then combining those beliefs into a general overall attitude toward the object. The most commonly used cognitive structure model in advertising is the evaluative belief model, in which the attitude is the sum of the evaluative beliefs about how well each brand scores on each attribute, weighted by the importance of that attribute:

$$A_0 = \Sigma w_d a_{0d}$$

Where,

A_0 = attitude of an individual or segment toward object o

w_d= measure of the relative importance or weight of attribute d to the individual or segment.

a_{0d}= evaluation of an individual or segment toward object o with respect to attribute or dimension d, the evaluative belief

(b) Using Cognitive Structure Models for Message Strategy

The model assumes that there are a limited number of known attributes with known weights. In some circumstances, a consumer may not be aware of all the attributes used. A consumer, for example, may rationalize the purchase of a small sporty convertible on the basis of gas mileage but actually buy it because of a subconscious drive to lead an exciting life. Further, the model assumes that the weighted evaluative beliefs are added when there could be interactions present. A person may want some combination of attributes and will not value the object highly unless the desired set of attributes is included.Another assumption is that a person first obtains belief information and then uses that information to alter attitudes. However, the process could actually work the opposite way.

(c) Ideal Point Models

There are dozens of other attitude models that are elaborations of the basic evaluative belief model. Some, such as ideal-point models, rely on different approaches to data collection and an assumption that a particular combination of levels on each attribute can be found that represents a person's or total market's "ideal" combination. The obvious message strategy implications of these models is to make the advertised brand seem perceptually closer to the ideal brand by using the positioning tactics.

(d) Non-Compensatory Models

The evaluative belief models we discussed are examples of compensatory models. A low rating on one dimension can be compensated for by a high rating on another dimension. There are also a set of non-compensatory models that might be better in certain situations. Three such models are the conjunctive, disjunctive, and lexicographic.

The **conjunctive model** emphasizes low ratings on the various attributes. An object will be deemed acceptable if it meets a minimum standard (a minimum attribute level) on each attribute. This process has been shown to operate in supermarket buying decisions. For example, new grocery products were considered for stocking by buyers only if they rated at least average in quality, company reputation, sales representation, and category volume and were less than 110 percent of the cost of the closest substitute. If they failed to meet any of these criteria, they were excluded. Similarly, one can imagine that a student buying a personal computer might have minimum requirements in terms of memory, chip speed, and so on. An advertiser must, in such situations, ensure that the ad's content does not make any "errors of omission" and present information about all the key attributes. For example, if target consumers want to buy PCs with at least 8 megabytes of RAM, they may ignore ads for brands that only offer 4 megabytes as standard, even if these computers can later be upgraded to more memory. It might make more sense to offer and advertise the PC with the desired minimum level of memory.

The **disjunctive model**stresses high ratings. It regards objects as positive only when they have been rated outstanding on one or more of the relevant attributes. For instance, ready-to-eat breakfast cereals have many attributes (such as taste, nutritional content, etc.), but there may some eaters of such cereals who care most about the cereal not getting soggy in milk. Thus a cereal advertiser advertising to them needs to ensure that advertising focuses on the "stays crispy" benefit.

The **lexicographic model** assumes that an individual will evaluate the brand on the most salient attribute. If two or more brands "tie" on this attribute, the evaluation will shift to the second most salient attribute. The process will continue until a brand is selected.

Research shows that some of these non-compensatory models (e.g., the lexicographic one) are often used when the consumer is not really very involved or is under time pressure to make a choice, so that choosing the very best brand is not the prime concern, just a brand that "is good enough." It is also quite possible that an individual in some contexts may use more than one model. He or she could, for example, use a conjunctive model to determine a set of brands to consider and then use a compensatory model to make the final decision. Clearly, the existence of such multimodel decision processes makes model evaluation more difficult.

(e) Category Evaluation Model

The implicit assumption of cognitive structure models is that products are made up of discrete attributes and the decision makers combine these attributes to form an overall product attitude. A very different approach is category-based evaluation, which is based on the premise that people often divide the world into categories. In evaluating a new stimulus, it is placed into a category, and the attitude toward that category is retrieved from memory and applied to the stimulus. Reactions toward an individual can result from matching up that individual to a person category and applying the established attitudes toward that category.

For the category-based evaluation approach to operate, consumers develop a set of expectations about the product category. This expectation can be represented by either a typical example of the category, a prototype, or by a good example of the category, an-exemplar.To implement an advertising strategy based on the category-based model, the advertising should focus on positioning the brand with respect to some category exemplar. There would be no effort to communicate explicitly at the attribute level. One example is the humorous advertising for Parkay margarine which has a voice coming out of a box saying "butter." The advertising serves to position margarine with butter.

6. Segmentation using Attitude Structure

When we talk about people's opinions in a group, we often average out their views. This means we assume that the group is somewhat similar in their thoughts, and the average opinion represents most of the group. But, in reality, people might agree on how well different brands perform in various ways, like saying a car is good on gas or that a brand is known for safety. However, they will likely have different opinions on how important these things are when they choose a product.

So, just looking at the average importance ratings for attributes in a market isn't very helpful. Instead, we should consider the differences in how important these attributes are to different people. These differences can help us create segments for advertising and marketing strategies.

For example, let's say you're in charge of advertising for Jio's long-distance phone service. Research might show that Jio is seen as a high-quality service with good reliability, customer service, and operator assistance compared to competitors. On the other hand, Airtel might be known for having lower prices. These perceptions could be similar among all customers. However, customers might have different opinions on how important these qualities are. Some might care more about lower prices and value that more, while others might prioritize quality, customer service, and operator assistance. These different groups are what we call "segments" in marketing.

IMPORTANT QUESTIONS

1. How can attitude be measured?
2. What are the various components of attitude?
3. What are the non-compensatory rules of measuring attitude?

❍ ❍ ❍

Chapter 11

WORD OF MOUTH

INTRODUCTION

According to Peter Drucker, business has only two basic functions-marketing and innovation. Innovative practices transform the approach of the organization towards its consumers. If consumers are satisfied, the business can attain prosperity. Existing ideas cannot be effective for the long run. Marketers should focus on the generation of new ideas to grab the opportunities.

WORD OF MOUTH

Word of Mouth (WOM) in advertising refers to the process where consumers share their opinions, experiences, and recommendations about a product or service with others. This communication happens informally and typically among friends, family members, or peers. WOM is a powerful tool in advertising because it is considered more credible and trustworthy than traditional advertising messages. It can significantly impact a brand's reputation and influence consumer decisions. Marketers often aim to stimulate positive WOM by providing exceptional products, service, and memorable experiences that encourage customers to become brand advocates and share their positive impressions with others.

Additionally, in the context of digital marketing and social media, WOM has evolved into electronic word of mouth (eWOM) or Word-of-mouse, where people share their opinions and recommendations online through social networks, reviews, and discussions. Managing and leveraging eWOM has become crucial for modern advertising strategies.Next, we discuss several characteristics that increase the likelihood of success of word-of-mouth communications:

1. Motivational Characteristics

Why do people talk to others about a product or an ad campaign? According to Ernest Dichter, there are motivations behind it. When someone talks about a product, it's often because they gain something from it, like satisfaction or a reward. In simpler terms, people talk about products that fulfill their needs or goals.There are four main reasons why people talk:

- **Product Involvement:** People like to talk about things that make them happy or unhappy. It's a way to share their experiences and confirm that they own something.
- **Self-Involvement:** People want validation for their decisions and seek attention. They might talk about a product to show off or feel superior.
- **Other Involvement:** Sometimes, people talk about products to help others and share the benefits of the product. It can express care, friendship, or love.
- **Message Involvement:** Advertising itself can trigger conversations. Ads can become the topic of discussions.

2. Opinion Leadership

Who are the kinds of people who have the most impact on others in such informational and word-of-mouth processes? The concept of the opinion leader is relevant here, and it has been a central focus for much empirical research in sociology and marketing.It is interesting to recall that Katz and Lazarsfeld first defined the concept as "leadership at its simplest," "almost invisible," at the "person-to-person level of ordinary, intimate, informal, everyday contact."John Myers, for example, found in the case of the adoption of new frozen-food products, in which the new products were given to "positive" and "negative" opinion leaders, that group opinions toward the new products tended to follow those of the opinion leader in both positive and negative cases.

One of the first questions that needs to be asked is whether opinion leadership is a general or a specific phenomenon. It is not at all clear that an opinion leader in one product class (e.g., fashionable clothes) also tends to be an opinion leader in another (e.g., personal computer equipment). From an advertiser's view: point, another important question is the degree to which opinion leaders are differentially responsive to advertising appeals.

3. Motivation for listening to opinion leaders

So far, we've discussed the people who share word-of-mouth messages. But what about those who listen? Who are they more likely to be? Well, when people listen to word-of-mouth, there are a couple of important things to consider.

First, the person who is recommending something should genuinely care about the listener and their well-being. Second, the speaker should know a lot about the product and have personal experience with it. These two factors make the recommendation more convincing.Trust is also a key factor here. The listener needs to trust the person who's talking.

There are seven types of people who can be influential when they share their opinions:

- Experts in the field (connoisseurs)
- People who share similar interests
- Those who are very close to you (intimates)
- Those with good intentions (people of goodwill)
- People who can show tangible evidence
- And, of course, those with authority and credibility in the commercial world, like experts, celebrities, and authorities in that particular field.

THE DIFFUSION PROCESS

Marketers are interested in knowing how consumers learn about new products and the decision-making process involved in adopting them. Adoption process may be defined as the mental process through which an individual passes from first hearing about an innovation to final adoption (Philip Kotler). So, adoption can be said to be the decision by an individual to become a regular user of the product.

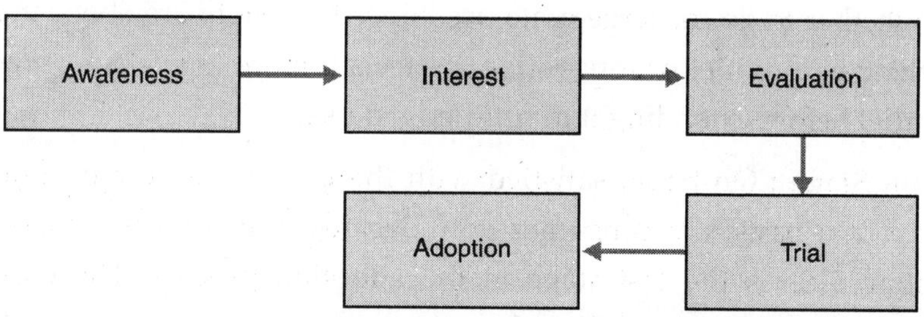

When marketers introduce a new product or an innovation to its target market, a lot of planning goes into managing the resistance to adopt the innovation. Because the adoption of an innovation is a process involving a change in buyer's attitude and perception. There are many stages involved right from when the consumer or potential consumer gets to know about the new product till, he finally consumes it or adopts it. Generally, the consumer goes through five stages in the process of adopting new products. The five stages are:

1. **Awareness Stage :** In this stage an individual comes to know about an innovation or new idea or new product/ service. He becomes aware of the innovation from any sources of information like friends or neighbor, co-workers, commercial sources etc. The individual only learns about the innovation from either of the sources of

information mentioned above. This means his knowledge about the innovation is only limited to the extent of the information generated by the source of information from where he first learns about the innovation.

2. **Interest Stage :** After being aware of the new product or innovation, in this stage, the consumer is stimulated and is interested in the innovation. He goes about seeking more information about the new product. He is interested in gathering more detailed information related to the innovation in terms of its utility aspects, its performance, durability and so on. The in-depth information sought by him will try to be obtained from all the sources he finds reliable.

3. **Evaluation Stage :** Based on the information gathered by the individual, he will evaluate and take a decision whether it is worthwhile and whether it will make sense and do him good to try out the innovation. In other words, from all the information collected by him related to the innovation, he will mentally try to evaluate the worthiness of the innovation. He will assign weights to the product attributes and work out to what extent the new product will be useful to him and then decide whether to try the new product.

4. **Trial Stage :** After evaluating the worthiness of the new product to him, the consumer may decide to try out the innovation on a small-scale basis initially to make an actual assessment of the value of the new product. He/she wants to experiment with the innovation and depending on how comfortable he feels with the product, he will decide whether to go for large scale use. Since he is not sure about the outcome of the use of the new product or innovation, he feels it more logical and practical to go for a sample trial before extending it to full-fledged usage.

5. **Adoption Stage :** On being satisfied with the use of the new product, purchased by him on a trial basis, the consumer now decides to make full and regular use of the innovation. This is the last stage in the adoption process. The consumer takes the decision to go for a full-fledged and continuous use of the new product or innovation.

ADOPTER CATEGORIES IN THE DIFFUSION PROCESS

It must be remembered that people vary remarkably in their readiness to try out new products or innovation. Everett M. Rogers has defined a person's innovativeness- as the degree to which an individual is relatively earlier in adopting new ideas than other members of his social system. Just as any product goes through a product life cycle, for each new product we can categorise adopters also. We can categorise adopters of the new products based on the relative time of their adoption of the innovations. This adoption process curve shape is almost similar to the PLC (product life cycle) of a product.

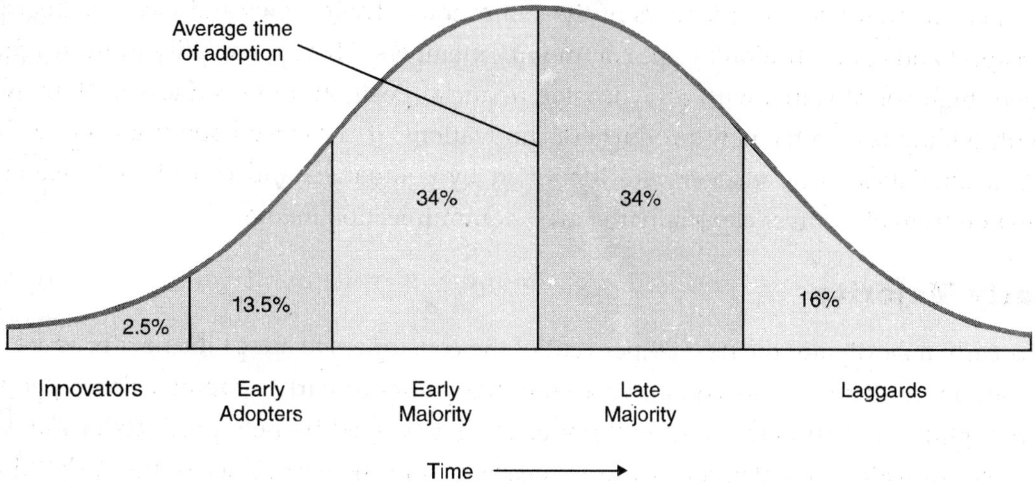

The above figure shows the diffusion process given the shape of a normal distribution curve when considered over a time. The process starts with a slow beginning, then picks up momentum with a greater number of persons adopting the innovation, then after a certain number reaching the peak, there is a decline with a smaller number of adopters remaining. A brief description of the category of adopters is given here under.

1. Innovators

After being aware of and seeking more information of new products, only 2.5 per cent of all the customers normally try out the new products. These people are referred to as the pioneers or innovators of the new product. Innovators are venturesome. They are easily acceptable to new ideas. They do not deliberate when new products are launched in the market. There is always a willingness on their part to try out new products even at the risk, that being the consumption pioneers, there is no feedback available on the use of the innovation from others. These people are usually found to be outgoing, gregarious, more educated and generally follow a life style matching the high social class 'status'. They consider it a chip to their shoulders when referred to as the innovators of the new product. Though, it may be remembered that this category of innovators of the new product is only a negligible 2.5 per cent of the entire target potential customers identified for the new product.

2. Early Adopters

The early adopters are the next 13.5 per cent of the buyers who adopt the new idea or new product. These people do not immediately plunge into buying as soon as a new product is available in the market. The early adopters also take to purchasing or trying the new product quite early but after carefully verifying and gathering information about the new idea or new product from authentic sources. Companies have identified that the early adopters are usually recognised as opinion leaders in their social circles or community. These people are looked upon with respect, as they are social leaders of the community. Their views and facts are heard with lot of respect and concentration by the community members. Their personality indicates them as educated, high social status with a favourable financial position, more successful than average and with willingness to try new products or innovations, if convinced about the same. Due to these characteristics early adopters are identified by companies and considerably exposed to information from all sources especially the mass communication media.

3. Early Majority

The early majority are the next 34 per cent of the consumers to adopt the new product. These people are more deliberate as compared to the innovators or early adaptors. These people are more thoughtful and shrewder and will not easily get swayed by new products or innovation. They prefer to wait and watch and learn by hearing from the experience of the early adopters, before thinking of adopting an innovation. They can be referred to as-the middle-class persons with reasonable education, occupation and income. These people, though rarely leaders, adopt new ideas before the average person. Once the innovation is adopted by this early majority of people, it ceases to be a luxury or a novelty item because it is an accepted fact that the early majority are deliberate in their behaviour to accept innovations.

4. Late Majority

The next 34 per cent of buyers of new products are referred to as the late majority to adopt the innovation. These people, unlike the earlier mentioned categories of adopters to the innovation, are more conservative in their approach and do not immediately respond in favour of a change. Their acceptance of the new product will come into effect only after a public opinion is in favour of the new product or innovation. The late majority are people with limited education, and have an average social status, drawing limited salary and consequently having limited purchasing power. They are more skeptical and will adopt an innovation only after most of the people have tried it.

5. Laggards

This is the last category of buyers to adopt a new product, comprising of 16 percent of the total market. As the term 'laggards' indicate, these are people who are lagging in their acceptance of an innovation. These people are very conservative, tradition bound and vary or are suspicious of changes. A lot of deliberation, caution and suspicion is exhibited in their buying behaviour for new products. They generally prefer to mingle with people who share a similar traditional outlook. They will adopt the innovation only because the innovation has taken a step in the direction of tradition.

The above-mentioned classification of adopters of a new product suggests that the firm introducing a new product should do research on the demographic, psychographic and media characteristics of innovators, and early adopters and specially work out communication programmes, directed at them. Understanding how a consumer seeks and processes information about new products and the decision-making process adopted by them can improve the adoption rate of new products. As seen above only 16 percent of all the customers, namely the innovators (2.5 per cent) and early adopters (13.5 per cent), normally try out new products soon after the launch. So, firms can exploit the natural tendency of this section by meeting their needs and accelerate the pace of acceptance. This is because, these segments endorsement of the product will have a positive impact in terms of appeal to the other categories of adopters comprising the 34 per cent of early majority, another 34 per cent of late majority and the remaining 16 per cent of the laggards.

Non-Adopter Categories

There is another opinion to include the category of non-adopters also, which will be in accordance with the marketplace reality, because not all potential consumers will necessarily adopt a product innovation. These are:

- **The unaware group** - Those consumers who are not aware of the new product
- **Symbolic-rejectors** - Who, though aware of the product, have decided against buying it.
- **Symbolic adopters**-Who know the product will be useful for them but have not tried it.
- **Trial adopters** - Who have tried the product but have not gone for a repurchase or actual purchase.
- **Trial rejectors** - Who have tried the product and rejected the same.

CASE STUDY: PAPERBOAT

Paper Boat established in 2013 by Hector Beverage, is fastest growing food and beverage company known for its ethnic drinks. The company serves an exclusive range of authentic traditional Indian beverages like Aam panna, Jaljeera, Neembu pani and many more. In a market dominated by soft drinks majors Coca Cola and PepsiCo, customers did not have the option of a drink that offered the traditional Indian taste and flavours. Paper Boat identified this gap and niche segment seeking the age-old traditional beverages with an authentic taste that seemed lost in the hustle-bustle of the urban lifestyle. The company aims to preserve the traditional beverage recipes of India using innovation to make its ethnic drinks free of artificial colouring or preservatives. Paper Boat follows clean and snazzy packaging design, unique for each product category, positioning the exclusivity of the brand with the help of an exceptional set of images and textures. Paper Boat has successfully deployed Intense digital marketing techniques based on creative storytelling focused on childhood nostalgia to connect with the target audience at a personal level. With its unique blend of success elements such as ethnic Indian flavoured beverages—the true hero of the Paper Boat's success story, its unique, eye-catching, and convenient packaging with snazzy look, and aggressive digital marketing communication based on stories capturing the deep emotions and childhood nostalgia, Paper Boat became one of the most popular Indian beverage brands. Staying ahead of health awareness trends, Paper Boat has firmly established itself as a valuable brand whit, still operating under the company's original mission —to create delicious, healthy, organic, beverages with honesty, integrity, and an eye toward sustainability.

IMPORTANT QUESTIONS

1. What do you understand by Word of Mouth advertising?
2. What is the difference between WOM and e-WOM?
3. Explain the diffusion process of adopting the innovative products.
4. Elaborate the adopter categories used in the diffusion process.

❍❍❍

Chapter 12

ART OF COPYWRITING

INTRODUCTION

Copywriting is an undeniable cornerstone of successful marketing endeavours, holding the power to make or break your campaigns. Whether you're weaving together persuasive sales copy, crafting captivating blog posts, or curating compelling social media content, mastering the art of copywriting is nothing short of essential.Copywriting is the art and science of crafting written content, such as advertisements, marketing materials, website copy, and more, with the primary goal of persuading the reader or viewer to take a specific action. This action could be making a purchase, signing up for a newsletter, clicking a link, or simply engaging more deeply with the content. Effective copywriting is a fundamental element of successful marketing and communication strategies.

A skilled copywriter understands how to use words to convey a message that not only captures the reader's attention but also resonates with their needs and desires. It involves employing persuasive language, storytelling, and various techniques to create content that is engaging, compelling, and persuasive. Successful copywriting is not just about using the right words; it's about understanding the audience, their pain points, and the unique selling points of the product or service. It involves testing and refining copy to optimize its effectiveness and may often incorporate elements like calls to action, headlines, subheadings, and the use of emotional appeal.In a digital age where content is abundant, copywriting remains a critical skill for businesses and individuals looking to stand out, connect with their target audience, and drive desired actions. A well-crafted piece of copy can be the difference between a successful marketing campaign and one that falls flat.

COPYWRITING Vs. ADVERTISEMENT WRITING Vs. CONTENT WRITING

Basis	Copywriting	Advertisement Writing	Content Writing
Primary Purpose	To persuade the reader or viewer to take a specific action like purchase or subscribe.	To promote a product, service, or idea and persuade the target audience to take a specific action (e.g. purchase, sign up etc.)	To inform, educate, or entertain an audience, providing valuable information, insights, or entertainment
Focus	Creating compelling and persuasive messages.	Crafting entire advertisements including copywriting and design	Providing information,insights, or engagement.
Audience	The audience is targeted and segmented, to perform a specific action.	Targeted audience with a specific message	Broad or niche audiencedepending on the topic.Varied, including blog
Form and Medium	Often found in short and impactful forms, such as headlines, slogans, jingles, and concise ad text, commonly used in advertising materials.	Various mediums such as print, digital, radio, TV, online and more.	Varied, including blog posts, articles, ebooks, social media posts, etc.
Tone and Style	Persuasive, creative and attention-grabbing.	Varied depending on the medium and message often catchy.	Informal, formal, or conversational, depending on the purpose and audience.
Goal	Drive a specific action such as purchase or subscription.	Promote a product, service or an idea	Inform, engage and possibly entertain the audience
Skills Required	Persuasive writing skills, marketing knowledge	Copywriting, visual design, marketing knowledge	String writing skills, research and SEO for online content
Examples	Advertising headlines, slogans, call-to-action, phrases etc.	TV commercials, print ads, online display ads, sponsored content.	Blog posts, articles, website content, social media post etc.

COPYWRITNG AND CREATIVITY

It is the job of the creative department of the agency to generate alternative advertisement ideas and ultimately to pick one or a few that will go forward into production. The creative department is made up of copywriters who have the main responsibility of creating the advertisement, and art directors having the expertise of creating or illustrations and pictorial material. The creation stage encompasses the creative *(idea generation)* process, the generation of written copy *(copywriting)* artwork of various kinds *(Illustrating)*,and a preliminary or comprehensive version of the advertisement *(layout)*.

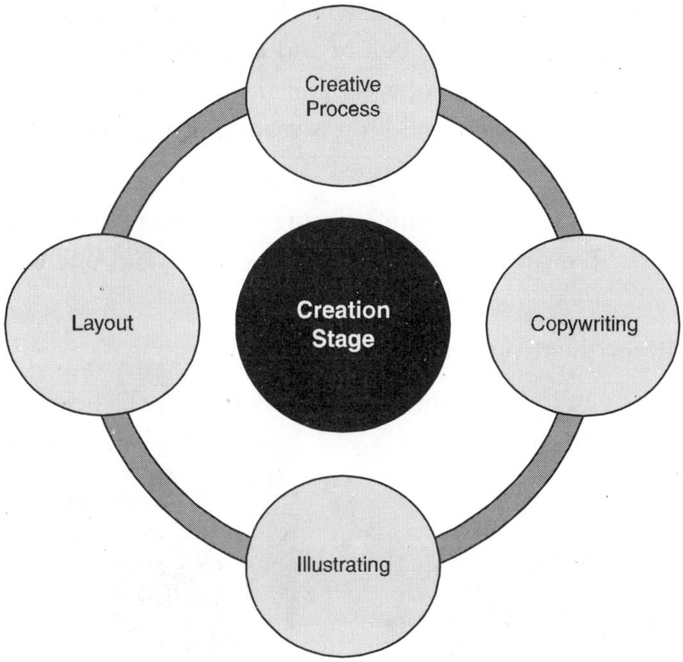

I. CREATIVE PROCESS

The creative process in marketing is the transformative stage where a raw marketing proposition, often born from marketing research and technical specifications, is evolved into one or more imaginative concepts. These creative ideas are crafted to communicate to the consumer clearly, powerfully, and persuasively what benefits the brand provides and why it should hold significance for them. The creative process picks up where research concludes, transcending the data-driven aspects of marketing. It bridges the analytical and technical aspects of marketing with the artistry and human touch needed to engage, captivate, and influence consumers effectively. It transforms a mere proposition into a compelling narrative or visual representation that resonates with the audience, leaving a lasting impact and prompting desired actions. The most common manifestation of the creative system is a series of steps that involve different types of thinking and problem-solving. These steps include:

A. **Preparation**: The preparation stage is the first stage of creativity, and it starts with gathering information and data, such as resources and ideas.

B. **Incubation**: The second stage, incubation, is where the creative idea is incubated in an environment without any pressure or stress. It's a period where one can free their mind from any distractions, allowing their thoughts to flow freely.

C. **Illumination**: The third stage, illumination, is when the work done in the first two stages come together. This is where one can begin developing a plan of action and a more concrete idea of the end result.

D. **Evaluation**: The evaluation stage can actually take place before or after the project. One might even opt to evaluate both before and after the implementation phase. In short, the evaluation stage is when one weighs the success of the stages, and also how developed the creative idea is - and if it is ready for implementation or publication - or if the idea needs to be recast or scrapped altogether.

E. **Implementation**: The implementation stage is when all of the ideas, plans, and evaluations from the previous stages come together, and one begins and finishes the project.

Example of a creative advertisement for "Amul Butter"

Ad Concept: "The Taste of India – Amul: The Utterly Butterly Delicious Story"

This advertisement celebrates Amul Butter as an integral part of India's culinary culture, spanning from rural households to high-end restaurants. It conveys a message of quality, tradition, and the irreplaceable role of Amul Butter in Indian cuisine. The use of traditional elements, a focus on real-life scenarios, and the iconic Amul girl create a memorable and emotionally resonant ad campaign.

II. COPYWRITING

Copywriting is the composition of headings, sub-headings and the body copy of advertisements, catalogues or brochures. Therefore, copywriters help promote businesses, ideas and opinions by writing advertisements for organisations. This is an art of writing and compiling creativity in writing content.

"WORDS HAVE THE POWER TO INFLUENCE READERS' PERCEPTIONS OF MESSAGES".

Copywriting is the skill of choosing the right words and technique of arranging them smartly to promote business, product, service, idea, or a person. The selection of words and its presentation largely depends upon the media through which it is planned to convey. For example, depending on whether it is a newspaper, magazine, hoarding, radio, television, or internet, the script will vary accordingly.However, whatever is the type of media, the purpose of copywriting is the same i.e. promotion. Therefore, it should be persuasive enough to be instantly attention grabbing.

Elements of Copywriting

- **Heading** – Headline gives the first impression and lasts on readers' mind, therefore, it should be eye-catching. Heading should tell – what it is all about your ad in a very few words, ranging from 3 to 30 words.
- **Body copy** – Write body copy in such a way that it seems as the continuity of the heading. Provide details of all the features and benefits that you are claiming for. The language should be promising and trustworthy.
- **Slogans** – Think of *"The ultimate driving machine"* (BMW); *"Just do it"* (Nike); *"Because I'm worth it"* (L'Oréal), what comes to your mind? The moment, you hear the slogans, you link it with the respective brand not only because you have heard it many times, but rather it works. A well-written and effective slogan is a trustworthy brand representative. However, your slogan should be small and crispy giving meaning to your brand.
- **Taglines** – Taglines are usually used for literary products to reinforce and strengthen the audience's memory of a literary product. For example: India ki apni dukaan - Amazon
- **Jingle Lyrics** – More often accompanied with background music, jingle lyric is a short slogan, tune, or verse written to be easily remembered (especially used in advertising). For example, **Amul- Amul doodh peeta hai India'**
- **Scripts** (for audio and video ad) –Scripts are the descriptions of an ad that narrates the dialogues, actions, expression, and movements of characters. Since, script is a complete guideline of an ad; therefore, it should be written meaningfully, orderly, and nicely.
- **Others** – (White Paper, Press Release, & other written material such as emails, articles, and blog (for the internet)): These are all promotional write-ups written purposefully to promote a particular product/service. So, while writing white paper, press release,

articles, blog, or even an email you need to focus or emphasize only on one product that you want to promote. You need to describe all features and offers of the respective product in simple and plain language.

Guidelines for copywriting:

The better the advertisement copy is, the more effective it should be to elicit a result such as a higher conversion rate. The writer must determine the optimum way to communicate with their audience. Following things should be kept in mind:

- Cash in your personal experience.
- Organise your experience.
- Write from your heart.
- Learn from the experiences of others.
- Talk with the manufacturer.
- Study the product.
- Review the previous advertisements of the product.
- Study competitors' advertisement.
- Study the testimonials from customers.
- Solve the prospect's problem.
- Put your subconscious mind to work.

III. Principles for Copywriting

1. General Copy Principles

Regardless of the specific ad medium, copy is usually more effective if it is simple, containing only one or two key ideas; contains a benefit or idea unique to the brand being advertised; is extendible (can lead to several variations in a campaign); and flows naturally and smoothly from beginning to end.Good ads are specific, using facts and figures and believable details instead of generalities.

One overriding rule for developing copy is to keep the format simple, uncluttered, and straightforward. Whether in print or in broadcast, the tendency for including too much information or for complicating the television commercial with too many scene changes, or scenes that are not well integrated, should be avoided. This principle of simplicity extends to the language used as well. Like cluttered format, complicated language is unlikely to induce people to spend the time to "figure it out." The message should always be true to the product. Claims should be sustainable and the style should not be radically altered over the life cycle of the product.

2. Print Copy Principles:

Effective print copy follows a set of fundamental principles that are instrumental in captivating and persuading the reader. These principles encompass a clear understanding of the target audience and their needs, an emphasis on simplicity and clarity, the creation of compelling headlines, storytelling to engage emotions, a focus on benefits over features, the inclusion of persuasive calls to action, and the use of social proof and urgency to drive action. Additionally, a conversational tone fosters a strong connection with the reader, while logical structure and thorough editing ensure the message is comprehensible and error-free. Embracing these principles enables print copy to convey messages with impact, encourage reader engagement, and guide them toward desired actions, ultimately contributing to the effectiveness of the marketing or communication efforts. Some guiding principles are as follows:

- Knowing the demographics, interests, pain points, and aspirations of the target audience which allows to tailor your message to resonate with them. Effective print copy speaks directly to the reader's needs and desires.
- Avoid complex jargon and convoluted sentences. Keep your message straightforward and concise.
- A compelling headline is the first point of contact between your content and the reader. It must grab their attention and awake their interest.
- Storytelling elements adds depth and emotional resonance to the print copy having a unique ability to connect with readers on a personal level, making your content memorable.
- Instead of focusing solely on features, emphasize the benefits of the product or service offers.Clearly communicate the value proposition.
- Every piece of print copy should include a strong and clear call to action i.e. indicating what to do next, purchase, subscribe or visiting a website.
- Incorporate social proof elements such as customer testimonials, endorsements, or case studies.
- Mentioning limited time offers or exclusive deals can drive conversions.
- Print copy is logically structured with a clear flow of ideas. Each section should naturally lead to the next, providing a coherent reading experience.
- Error-free copy communicates professionalism and attention to detail.

3. Outdoor Copy Principles

Outdoor advertising, often seen on billboards, transit ads, and posters, demands a distinct set of principles to engage viewers on the move. These principles prioritize simplicity, clear messaging, and high-impact visuals. In the limited time available, an outdoor ad must convey its message swiftly, utilize eye-catching imagery and minimal text, and inspire immediate action. Effective outdoor copy respects the importance of location, ensuring relevance to the surroundings and target audience. It often relies on memorable slogans, vivid graphics, and a strong call to action, motivating passersby to recall and respond to the message.High-impact visuals are essential to catch the viewer's eye. The use of bold colours, striking images, and creative design elements can make the ad stand out amidst a cluttered urban environment.Effective outdoor copy grabs attention, delivers a memorable message, and encourages immediate action. It's a dynamic and impactful form of advertising, often with a unique set of constraints and opportunities compared to other media.

4. Retail Copy Principles

Effective retail copy is all about understanding your customers and delivering clear, concise messages. It should highlight product benefits, communicate promotions, and include compelling calls to action. Visual appeal plays a crucial role, especially in e-commerce. Transparency in pricing, social proof, and the art of storytelling build trust. SEO considerations are essential for online retail, and data-driven decisions through testing and analytics are vital. Mobile-friendliness and consistency across channels strengthen brand identity. Additionally, seasonal relevance keeps your messaging current and engaging. By following these principles, retailers can create persuasive and customer-centric copy that boosts sales and fosters customer loyalty, whether in-store or online.

5. Business to Business Ads

B2B ads target businesses and should address their specific needs and challenges. They emphasize value propositions, trust, and data-driven content. B2B advertising often requires longer sales cycles, educational materials, and personalization for different roles within the business. A multi-channel approach, strong calls to action, and relationship-building are crucial, along with consistency in brand messaging. Adapting to industry trends is essential in this evolving field. Effective B2B advertising builds trust, provides clear solutions, and fosters long-term business relationships.

6. Advertising through Internet

Advertising on the internet, often referred to as online advertising, is a dynamic and versatile marketing approach. It leverages the vast reach and interactivity of the internet to promote products, services, or brands. Internet advertising encompasses various formats, including display ads, social media ads, search engine marketing, video ads, and more. It offers precise targeting capabilities, allowing businesses to reach specific demographics, interests, or behaviours, which is particularly valuable for connecting with the right audience. Additionally, internet advertising provides real-time analytics, enabling advertisers to track the performance of their campaigns and make data-driven optimizations. Its flexibility, reach, and measurable results make online advertising a powerful tool for businesses to connect with their target audience and drive engagement, conversions, and brand awareness in the digital landscape.

IV. ILLUSTRATING

Illustrating in marketing and advertising plays a critical role in conveying messages and making brands memorable. It involves visual elements such as logos, images, and design choices, and decisions about what identification marks to include. These identification marks generally fall into one of three categories:

1. **Company or Trade Name:** The company's primary name, such as "Del Monte" or "Levi Strauss," often serves as a prominent identification mark. It plays a major role in reinforcing the brand identity and connecting the products or services to the parent company.
2. **Brand Name:** In some cases, specific products or product lines may have their own distinct brand names. These brand names can be used as identification marks to differentiate and promote individual offerings, even if they are part of a larger company.
3. **Trademarks:** Trademarks represent unique symbols, phrases, or designs that are legally registered to protect a company's intellectual property. They are a crucial part of branding and can be used as identification marks to signify the origin and quality of products.

The choice of which identification marks to include in advertising is driven by the branding and marketing strategy. For example, in a family-branding strategy, where a company wants to leverage its overall brand reputation, the company name (e.g., Del Monte) will prominently feature in advertisements. This approach aims to capitalize on the established trust and recognition of the parent company.

In contrast, some advertising campaigns may not even mention the company name or choose to deemphasize it. This approach is common in cases where individual product lines or brands have distinct identities and customer bases. For example, Proctor & Gamble may focus on promoting specific detergent brands without prominently featuring the parent company name in their advertisements.

Thus illustrating and choosing the right identification marks in advertising are strategic decisions that depend on the company's branding goals, the relationships between different brands and the parent company, and the target audience's preferences and expectations. These decisions significantly influence how consumers perceive and interact with a brand and its products or services.

V. LAYOUT

The layout in advertising refers to the visual arrangement of elements within an advertisement, whether it's for print, digital, or any other medium. A well-designed layout is crucial in capturing the audience's attention, conveying the message effectively, and driving the desired response.The layout of an advertisement is a critical element in conveying the intended message and making a lasting impact on the audience. Effective design and layout can set the tone for the brand, facilitate engagement, and drive the desired action, whether it's a purchase, a sign-up, or another response. Following principles must be kept in mind while deciding about the layout of an advertisement:

Principles of Good Layout

1. Focus on Dominant Element.
2. Unity of All AD Parts.
3. Good Use of Contrast.
4. Right Balance of Elements.
5. Maintain Proportion of Space.
6. Follow the Eye Movement.
7. Simple and Uncomplicated Layout.
8. Ease of Readability.
9. Use of Whitespace.
10. Clarity of AD Message.
11. Good Ad Background or Atmosphere.
12. Long Lasting First Impression.

TYPES OF TELEVISION COMMERCIALS

Audio and visual elements can be combined to produce several types of television commercials. TV commercials are the most prominent kind of television advertising and are supposed to be really good for target marketing while overlays are really useful for news channels. In spite of great competition from OTT and other digital formats, television advertising is still a dominant mode of advertising. Television advertising is a fairly flexible option for advertisers. Based on their budget and preferences, advertisers can either provide the tv channel an advertisement or have the channel create one for them. They can also choose between different times for the airing of the ad based on their target audience and budget. Television advertising avails quality customer engagement, a wide reach, high frequency, and a lasting impact to your advertisement

TV commercials come in various types and formats, each tailored to achieve specific advertising goals. Here are some common types of TV commercials:

1. **Product or Service Advertisements:** These are the most typical commercials, where a product or service is directly promoted. They often showcase the features and benefits of the offering and may include demonstrations or testimonials.
2. **Branding or Image Commercials:** These commercials aim to build brand awareness and shape the overall image of a company or product. They focus on conveying the brand's values, mission, and identity rather than specific products.
3. **Direct Response Advertisements:** These commercials encourage immediate viewer action, such as making a phone call, visiting a website, or making a purchase. They often include special offers and clear calls to action (CTAs).
4. **Comparison or Competitive Ads:** These commercials directly compare a brand's product or service with a competitor's, highlighting the advantages of their offering. They aim to sway viewers' preferences.
5. **Testimonial or Endorsement Ads:** Testimonial commercials feature real customers or celebrity endorsements sharing positive experiences with a product or service. This builds trust and credibility.
6. **Humour Ads:** Humorous commercials use humour to capture viewers' attention and entertain them while conveying a message. These ads are memorable and can create a positive association with the brand.
7. **Emotional Ads:** Emotional commercials aim to tug at viewers' heartstrings, elicit strong emotions, and create a connection with the brand. They often feature touching stories or societal issues.
8. **Slice-of-Life Ads:** These ads depict relatable everyday scenarios to show how a product or service fits into consumers' lives, making them identify with the brand.

9. **Dramatization Ads:** These commercials use dramatic storytelling to illustrate the impact of a product or service. They often create a problem-and-solution narrative.
10. **Infomercials**: Longer-form commercials, often ranging from 30 minutes to an hour, designed to educate viewers about a product or service in-depth, typically with demonstrations and customer testimonials.
11. **Public Service Announcements (PSAs):** PSAs aim to raise awareness or educate the public about important issues or causes. They are often used for social or charitable campaigns.
12. **Sponsorship Ads:** These ads appear at the beginning or end of a TV show, acknowledging a company's sponsorship of the program. They may include brief branding messages.
13. **Teaser or Trailer Ads:** Teasers and trailers are commonly used for movies, TV shows, or upcoming events to generate excitement and anticipation.

CREATIVE STYLES

> "Creativity without strategy is called art. Creativity with strategy is called advertising." – **Jef Richards.**

Creative advertising is a form of marketing that uses original concepts, designs, and storytelling to effectively communicate a message or promote a service or product. The most important and relevant creative styles used in the past and relevant today are as follows:

1. David Ogilvy's Style: The Brand Image

David Ogilvy, often referred to as the "Father of Advertising," was a renowned advertising executive known for his insightful principles on building strong brand images. One of his key contributions was emphasizing the importance of creating and maintaining a distinct and compelling brand image.David Ogilvy's principles on brand image have had a profound and lasting impact on the advertising industry. Today, his legacy is reflected in the way brands strategically craft and maintain their image to connect with consumers and create enduring brand loyalty.Here are seven of his timeless lessons about branding:

(i) **You can control how the market sees your brand:** "Every advertisement should be thought of as a contribution to the complex symbol which is the brand image."Brand image is the perception of a brand by the market, measured by its strength, which can be seen in market share over time. Brands are long-term concepts that require development, promotion, and support through aligned marketing activities. A weak brand image is a starting point for marketers but can be enhanced through promise delivery and customer support. A strong brand, characterized by a large market share and loyal customers, requires significant effort to discredit.

(iii) Focus on the product, but also make it attractive: Never underestimate the capability of the consumer to determine if your product is worth their money. If you think it's only the marketing that works, wait till your market uses your product and discovers it does not deliver its promise. The result? A disaster. Word-of-mouth can be more powerful than your best ad, especially if what the market has to say about the product is negative. This will certainly affect the brand image. Still, consider physical attractiveness. Create packaging that will catch the eye of your target market. Although it's more usual to over-emphasize packaging, there's no harm in making sure it captures attention.

Do not mislead your market"The consumer isn't a moron; she is your wife." Misleading the market in an ad qualifies as false advertising. Remember that nothing good comes out of it. Maybe it can produce a positive instant effect, as in a positive income right after the ad has been shown, but it will not strengthen your brand. The safest strategy, not to say the winning, is to create a product that your market deserves and that they can discern good products from the bad. Attune your marketing activities based on this idea and many will favour your brand.

(iv) Always set your branding apart: It is true that a successful and cutting-edge advertising campaign could tempt you to tailor yours, even slightly, to such campaign. It may work for a while, much to the annoyance of the owner of the original idea, but it will harm your brand image in the long run. How? Here's one way. Because your campaign takes after the original one, your brand gradually takes after the other brand or worse, it becomes just one of the brands. Take global brands Nike and Adidas for example. They have the same target market, but have you ever seen them create similar-sounding ads? No, because what one does is create a campaign that is better than the last and above the other's.

(v) Know your product: Know every facet of the product or service before you create an ad campaign. This allows you to understand the product and sell it well, not just by highlighting a characteristic that appeal to a target market, but by knowing that the product addresses a market's needs and wants. However, if you ignore this important step in advertising, you could make the mistake of promising something your product cannot deliver. Or, you fail to see why your product is better than its competitors. You don't only waste resources here, but you somehow harm or neglect the brand image.

(vi) Base your marketing strategy from experience: If you want to capture the interest of your target market, create an ad that situates your product in their lives. These appeal better to the emotion, which often becomes the basis for buying a product. If you think you don't know enough about your target market to create such an ad, do some research. Spend time observing their behaviour, their collective interest, and how they spend their free time.

(vii) **Make money from talent:** "In the modern world of business, it is useless to be a creative, original thinker unless you can also sell what you create."

This translates to, vaguely, as creating something that is not just creative and unique, but also engaging. In the realm of art, there is the concept of "creating art for the sake of art," rather than creating something that can be used. While it serves its own purpose among artists and those who appreciate such art, this notion obviously does not apply in marketing and advertising, where creative, original thinkers who could sell a product are immensely rewarded.

2. William Bernbach : Execution

William Bernbach was a legendary figure in the advertising industry known for his innovative and creative approach to advertising execution. He co-founded the advertising agency Doyle Dane Bernbach (DDB) and played a pivotal role in shaping modern advertising. William Bernbach's legacy is seen in the creative and human-cantered approach to advertising execution that continues to influence the industry. His work at DDB produced iconic campaigns and forever changed the way advertising is conceived and executed.

His approach to execution can be summarized as follows:

(i) **Creativity and Innovation:** Bernbach believed in pushing the boundaries of creativity in advertising. He encouraged the use of wit, humor, and unexpected approaches to capture the audience's attention and create memorable ad campaigns.

(ii) **Visual Storytelling:** He understood the power of visuals in conveying messages. Bernbach emphasized the importance of imagery and design in advertising execution to complement and enhance the message.

(iii) **Simplicity:** Bernbach advocated for simplicity in advertising. He believed that effective communication should be clear and straightforward, avoiding unnecessary complexity.

(iv) **Emotion and Connection:** He recognized the importance of emotional appeal in advertising. Bernbach's execution often aimed to create a strong emotional connection between the brand and the audience.

(v) **Human-Centered:** Bernbach's advertising focused on people and their experiences. He believed that understanding human behavior and psychology was essential to creating resonant advertising.

(vi) **Respect for the Consumer:** Bernbach's approach was respectful of the intelligence and discernment of consumers. He avoided talking down to the audience and treated them as intelligent individuals.

(vii) **Champion of Copywriters and Art Directors:** He valued the partnership between copywriters and art directors, recognizing that their collaboration was essential in creating impactful and memorable ads.

3. Leo Burnett: The Common Touch

Leo Burnett was a prominent figure in the advertising industry known for his philosophy of "The Common Man" and "The Common Touch." This approach emphasized creating advertising that resonated with everyday people and connected on a personal level. His "The Common Touch" philosophy left a significant mark on the advertising industry. It emphasized the importance of empathy, authenticity, and relatability in creating advertising that truly connects with people. His agency, Leo Burnett Worldwide, continues to uphold these principles in advertising campaigns around the world.

Here's what "The Common Touch" represented in Leo Burnett's advertising philosophy:

(i) **Empathy and Understanding:** Burnett believed in understanding the needs, desires, and challenges of the average consumer. He stressed the importance of putting oneself in the shoes of the common person to create relatable advertising.

(ii) **Simplicity and Clarity:** "The Common Touch" promoted simple and straightforward messaging. Burnett believed that clear, jargon-free communication was essential for making a genuine connection with the audience.

(iii) **Honesty and Authenticity:** Burnett's advertising valued authenticity and honesty. He believed that truthful advertising, which genuinely reflected a product's benefits, would resonate with consumers and build trust.

(iv) **Storytelling:** Burnett understood the power of storytelling in advertising. He encouraged the use of narratives that people could relate to and remember, creating emotional connections with brands.

(v) **Emotion and Humor:** He recognized the role of emotions and humor in advertising. Burnett's ads often evoked laughter, joy, or nostalgia, fostering a positive brand perception.

(vi) **Relatability:** Burnett's advertising aimed to be relatable to the common person's daily life and experiences. His work often featured everyday situations, characters, and relatable scenarios.

(vii) **Human-Centered Approach:** "The Common Touch" placed people at the heart of advertising. Burnett believed that advertising should focus on human needs and aspirations, rather than on merely pushing products.

(viii) Inclusivity: His approach was inclusive, aimed at connecting with a broad audience rather than a niche. The advertising spoke to a wide range of consumers, making them feel valued and understood.

4. Philip Dusenberry: Entertainment and Emotion

Philip Dusenberry was a celebrated figure in the advertising industry known for his emphasis on creating emotionally engaging and entertaining advertising. His legacy in advertising is seen in the emotionally charged and entertaining campaigns he created. His work often captured the essence of human experiences, making the brands he promoted more relatable and memorable. His approach continues to influence the industry by highlighting the power of entertainment and emotion in advertising.

His approach to advertising execution can be summarized as follows:

(i) Entertainment Value: Dusenberry believed that advertising should not only convey a message but also entertain the audience. He understood that entertaining ads are more likely to capture and hold viewers' attention, making the brand message more memorable.

(ii) Storytelling: Dusenberry was a proponent of using storytelling as a central element in advertising. He believed that well-crafted narratives could connect with consumers on an emotional level, making the ad more compelling and relatable.

(iii) Emotionally Charged: He recognized the power of emotions in advertising. Dusenberry's approach often aimed to evoke strong emotions in viewers, whether it was humour, nostalgia, sentimentality, or excitement. Emotional ads tend to create a lasting impact.

(iv) Music and Sound: Dusenberry understood the role of music and sound in creating an emotional connection. He often incorporated memorable music and soundtracks in his ads to enhance their impact and resonance.

(v) Simplicity and Clarity: Despite his focus on emotion and entertainment, Dusenberry believed in delivering the brand message with clarity and simplicity. He understood that viewers should readily grasp the main idea of the ad.

(vi) Relatability: Dusenberry's ads were often relatable to people's everyday lives, experiences, and aspirations. He aimed to create a connection between the brand and the common person.

(vii) Cultural Relevance: He recognized the importance of cultural relevance and often incorporated cultural references or themes into his advertising to make it more relatable to the audience.

(viii) Memorability: Dusenberry's ads were designed to be memorable. Whether through catchy slogans, jingles, or unforgettable visuals, he aimed to leave a lasting impression on viewers.

IMPORTANT QUESTIONS

1. What is copywriting and how it is different from advertisement writing and content writing?
2. "Creativity is interwoven in copywriting". Justify this statement in light of various elements of copywriting.
3. What is creative process? And how it is important in creating an advertisement?
4. Explain in detail the copywriting, its principles and the necessary guidelines to frame an advertisement copy.
5. Explain the types of TV commercials and the contribution of different creative styles in framing the advertisement.

❍ ❍ ❍

Chapter 13

MEDIA BUDGET

INTRODUCTION

Advertising is a billion-dollar industry. Most of the companies these days perceive advertising as an investment and spend millions on it to create brand equity which in turn generates huge profits for the firms. In 2017 alone, the amount spent on advertising by some of the leading companies was: Procter and Gamble - 7.12 billion US dollars, General Motors – 3.24 billion US dollars, Verizon – 2.64 billion US dollars in United states alone. As most companies spend a good fortune on advertising budgets, it is imperative to understand the tactics related to setting an advertising budget as one need to strategically evaluate where one can spend and where one can save.

DEFINITION AND OBJECTIVES

An Advertising Budget refers to the amount of money allocated towards advertising of a brand or a product. Advertising budget includes money for conducting advertising research, getting creatives made, printing material, allocating money to advertising media and ensuring proper implementation of ad campaigns.

While developing an advertising strategy, it is pragmatic to set advertising objectives which are notably influenced by the advertising budget. This is because advertising objectives are important for decision making and to have a standard against which the results can be measured. An organization may choose a sales objective or communication objective for the purpose of developing an advertising budget.

Sales Objectives

A sales objective is to increase the sales of products or to compliment the selling efforts of the sales department. The objective may be changed from time to time influenced by the volume of sales which may depend on –

- Price of products
- Advertising and Promotion
- Personal selling
- Competition
- Consumer tastes
- Product quality
- Economy
- Technology
- Direct action advertising

Communication objective

A communication objective is to create awareness, develop interest or to change an attitude. For this purpose, a business may choose to –

- Increase the percentage of target customers who associate a special feature or benefit with company's brand
- Increase number of customers who prefer company's brand over competing brands
- Increase company's brand usage among existing members
- Encouraging a brand trial among targeted customers

APPROACHES TO ADVERTISING BUDGET

There are two approaches to setting advertising budget:

Top-down approach

It is known as the top-down approach because the budgets are made by the top management and then, the money is passed down the line to various departments.

Build up approach

In this, promotion objectives are set for the tasks to be performed. All the necessary activities to achieve the objectives are planned by ascertaining and **setting**the cost of these activities. The total advertising budget is then approved by top management.

Top-Down Approach	Build Up Approach
Top management sets the spending limit	Advertising objectives are set by the managers which are later approved by the management
Advertising budget is set within the allocation limits.	Activities necessary to achieve objectives are planned
Advertising objectives and activities are planned according to the set budget.	Costs of different advertising elements are budgeted.
It is a Judgmental Approach	Total advertising budget is approved by top management
Budget is not linked to the objectives. This leads to predetermined budget allocations which are not related to advertising objectives.	Budget is allocated on the basis of activities considered essential to accomplish the objectives.
Methods – Affordable Method, Arbitrary Allocation, Percentage of Sales, Competitive parity, Return on investment	Methods – Objective and Task Method, Payout Planning, Quantitative Approach, Experimental Approach

TOP-DOWN APPROACH

I. The affordable method (All you can afford)

This is not a method to set advertising budget, in the real sense. The method is based on the company's potential to spend. The affordable method for setting an advertising budget is the simplest method of all and is also called the fund available method. This method of budgeting is based on the capacity of the firm to spend on advertising activities. As per this method, the firm goes for collecting funds for advertising only after all other expenses are met. It stands on the notion that any of the companies shouldnot spend more money on advertising beyond its capacity. If the after all expenses, some portion of money remains company goes for advertising, if not company goes without advertising.

Advantages:

1. It is simple.
2. It is flexible. This method is most fitting to individual requirements of the

organizations. In each case the profitability, the liquidity and the growth possibilities are of its own and can be decided appropriately.

3. When nothing can be known about the effects of advertising, top management sets a reasonable limit on the gamble.

Limitations:

1. This method completely ignores the role of advertising in the competitive market environment.
2. In the long run, it leads to uncertain planning as there is no guarantee that the company will spend money on advertising.
3. Except for an organization's financial position, other factors like an organization's need for advertising, consumer base, competition, and so forth are ignored.
4. This is not a method in the real sense.
5. There is possibility of bias in deciding advertising amount.

II. Arbitrary allocation method

This method seems to be a weaker method than the affordable method for setting an advertising budget. The arbitrary allocation method is completely dependent on the top management's discretion and hence, has no theoretical base. The budget is determined by management solely based on what they feel to be necessary. So ultimately the decision depends on the psychological and economic perspective of the people in the management and not on the market requirements.

The arbitrary allocation approach has following disadvantages:

1. There has been no systematic thinking
2. No objectives have been budgeted for
3. The concept and purpose of advertising and promotion have been largely ignored.

It is thus understood that the manager feels that some money must be spent on advertising and promotion and that is why he picks up an amount which has no logical explanation. Surprisingly, there are many companies both large and small, profit making and non-profit making, who continue to set their budgets this way.

III. Percentage of sales method

This is the most used method for budget setting. Large organizations generally go by this method. According to this method, advertising budget is based on sales of the product. Management determines the amount by either:

(i) taking a percentage of the historical or projected sales revenue.

(ii) Assigning a fixed amount of the unit product cost to promotion and multiplying this amount by the number of units sold.

- Some companies, instead of considering the past sales examine the percentage-of-projected future sales as a base. In the straight-percentage method, the marketing manager estimates projected sales for the coming year. The budget is a percentage of these sales, which is often an industry standard rate. In other words, a fixed percentage of last year's sales figure is allocated as the budget.
- For example, suppose the total sales of a company P Pvt. Ltd. in 2023-24 were ₹ 90, 00,000. The advertising budget is 20% of sales. So, the advertisement budget for the year 2024-25 is 20% of ₹ 90, 00,000 i.e. ₹18,00,000
- In case the ad budget is to be decided based on sales units, let us assume that the manufacturing cost per unit of table fan for P Pvt. Ltd. is ₹1,500 and the advertising money allocated per unit is Rs 100. The projected sales figure is 2,00,000 fans for the coming year 2024-25, then the total advertising budget can be calculated as ₹ 2,00, 000 x 100 = 2,00,00,000).

The percentage figure selected isusually a standard percentage across any industry. This figure varies from one industry to the other andbetween different firms in the same industry and depends on the organization's policy. Actual money spent varies considerably depending on the individual organization's total sales figure.

Sometimes the budget for the current year depends on the sales of the last year. Now if an organization keeps the percentage fixed and then the sales this year decrease, the advertising budget for next year is less. But marketing says that if the sales are fewer in a year one way out of many to increase it in the next year could be an increase in the promotional budget.

Thus, one advantage of using future sales as a base is that the budget is not based on last year's sales. As the market environment changes, management should consider the effect of these changes on sales in next year's forecast rather than relying on past data.

Advantages:

1. It is financially safe and helps an organization to keep advertising spending within limits irrespective of the fact whether the base is past year's sales or what the organization expects to sell in the upcoming year.
2. This method is simple, straightforward, and easy to implement.
3. It is not difficult to arrive at the calculations regardless of the basisused (whetherpast or future sales).

4. This budgeting approach is stable when competing organizations spend approximately the same percentage of their sales on promotion.

5. It encourages management to think of the relationship between promotion cost, selling price and profit per unit.

Disadvantages:

1. The basic premise on which the budget is established is sales. If the level of sales determines the amount of advertising and promotions to be spent, then the cause-and-effect relationship between advertising and sales is reversed as advertising is treated as an expense associated with making sales rather than an investment.

2. The percentage ofsales method of budgeting may result in misappropriation of funds i.e., over budgeting or under budgeting. When sales decrease, we may need more budget foradvertising as a decrease in budget might lead to further decrease in incremental sales.

3. This method is also difficult to use for new product introductions because in this case there is no sales history available. If the product is highly innovative and new in the market, projections of future sales may be difficult.

- **Marlboro**: Marlboro cigarettes were introduced in the 1920s. The brand share was only one per cent in the early 1950s. The company invested heavily in building brand image in 1954 (cowboy country) and now the brand share among young smokers is more than 60% in the USA.

- **Glaxo**: When Glaxo introduced Zantac (Zinetac in India), the medication for gastric ulcer, it was forecasted to gain no more than 10% share against the well-established Tagamet. Glaxo's investment-driven campaign helped Zantac achieve more than 50% share and it became the leading brand.

IV. Competitive parity method:

This method involves setting budgets to match competitors' outlays and funds. In this method, the organization monitors competitors' advertising and follows it. This method is generally used in markets in which advertising is heavier and the organization does not want to be left behind the competitors.

Normally, it is felt that the brand leader needs to spend proportionately less as a share of total advertising to maintain its market share, while a brand trying to improve its market share will have to spend proportionately more. But this type of budgeting plan fails to reflect the firms' own advertising needs or marketing requirements. None of the marketing managers in practice ever will accept the fact that they set their advertising and promotions budgets on the basis of what their competitors allocate. But a close examination of their advertising expenditures, both as a percentage of sales and in respect to the media where they are allocated, will show little variation in the percentage-of-sales figures for organizations within a given industry.

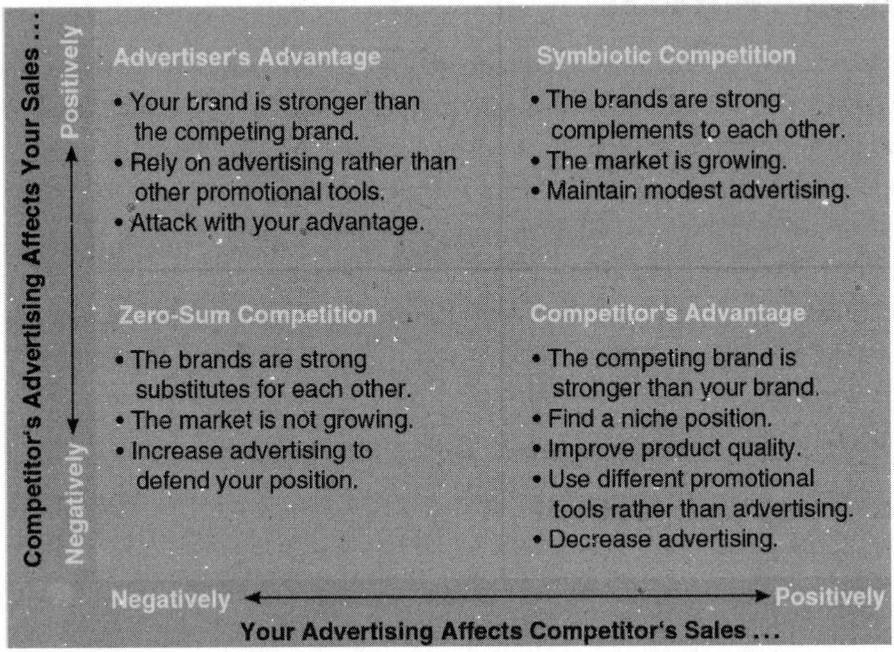

The logic for setting the budget this way is that the collective wisdom of the industry is involved. Some are of the opinion that since it takes competition into consideration, the marketplace is more stable and marketing war is minimized in turn minimizing the unrealistic ad expenditures. However, there are a number of **disadvantages** with this method:

1. It ignores the fact that advertising and promotions are designed to accomplish specific objectives and not merely to face competition.
2. It presumes that the ad campaigns will be equally effective because firms have made similar expenditures. This highly overlooks the contributions of creative executions and/or media allocations.
3. It disregards a very natural possibility that some organizations simply make better products than others.
4. There is no guarantee that competitors will not increase or decrease its own expenditures, regardless of what other organizations do because competition cannot be fully assessed at the beginning of a financial year.
5. Finally, there is no reason why competitive parity can and should avoid promotional wars. We are witnesses to the Coke versus Pepsi wars.

Nevertheless, companies employ the competitive parity method. But a wiser decision is not to overlook the competition but use this method in conjunction with the percentage-of-sales or other methods.

V. Return on investment

In the percentage-of-sales method, advertising budget is influenced by the level of sales. But advertising causes sales. So, the advertisement budget should be considered as an investment. In the ROI budgeting method, advertising and promotions are considered investments, just like plant and equipment. In other words, investments in advertisements lead to certain returns. Like other aspects of the firm's efforts, advertising is expected to earn a certain return. To many the ROI method is a supreme method of setting advertisement budget. But in reality, it is hardly possible to assess the returns provided by the promotional effort-at least as long as sales continue to be the basis for evaluation.

BUILD UP APPROACH

I. Objective and task method

In this method the selling objectives and budget decision are linked and considered simultaneously. It involves –

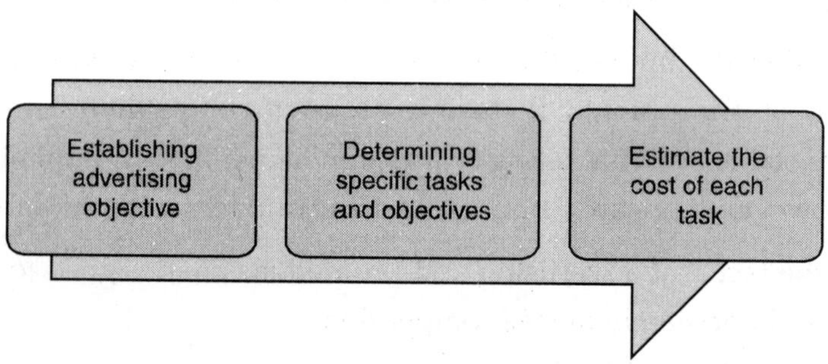

- Defining the advertising communication objectives to be accomplished
- Deciding specific strategies and tasks necessary to achieve them
- Estimating the costs involved in putting these activities in operation
- The total of these costs is taken as the base to determine the advertising budget.

Establishing objectives may be interpreted as achieving a percentage market share and bringing awareness of the brand to the consumers and general public. The strategies may include advertising in various media, and other elements of promotion mix. Then, the cost of various advertising media chosen is estimated. It is also necessary to monitor the expenses and evaluate the results. It is challenging to correlate the expenses with the task performed for this experience is required.

Advantages

1. The method develops budget from ground up which is a proper managerial approach.
2. It does not rely on past sales or future sale forecasts.
3. It considers all factors under advertiser's control.

Disadvantages

1. It is difficult to implement.
2. It requires managerial involvement and high skills.
3. It attempts to introduce variables such as awareness, knowledge, attitude formation etc.
4. It is difficult to estimate all costs and determine all tasks necessary to achieve the set objectives.

II. Payout planning method

It is practical when introducing a new product. The aim is to spend heavily to attain increased awareness and product acceptance. It estimates the investment value of advertising by linking it with other budgeting methods. The idea is to estimate the amount of revenue the product will generate and the costs it will incur over a period. The advertising budget is fixed on the rate of return desired, accuracy of sales forecast, factors affecting market, and estimated costs.

The advertiser determines the investment value of the advertising appropriation. The basic idea is to estimate the revenues the product will generate, as well as the costs it will incur, over a period of time, generally two to three years. Based on an expected rate of return, the payout plan will assist in determining how much advertising and promotions expenditures will be necessary when the return might be expected.

Advantages

It is useful and logical planning tool

Disadvantages

It cannot account for uncontrolled factors e.g. – competition, changes in government policies, new technology.

III. Quantitative models

Advertisers use quantitative methods including computer simulation models such as mathematical and statistical models to allocate advertising budget. Multiple regression analysis is used to govern the influence of advertising expenditure on sales. Experimentation and formal analysis is required to utilize this method. It is a time consuming and expensive method.

IV. The Experimental approach

It is a substitute to quantitative models. The Advertising manager conducts tests or experiments in one or more selected market areas to test the advertising strategy in these areas with similar population, brand usage, market share. Different advertising expenditure levels are kept for each market. Brand knowledge and sales levels are measured before and after. Results are compared and variation of influence of advertising expenditure studied. The feedback results determine the advertising budget levels. Managers may decide a certain budget level according to the advertising objectives.

Thus, these are the various methods of appropriating the advertising budget and by using these methods in combination, the advertisers can arrive at a more accurate and useful budget.

FACTORS AFFECTING ADVERTISING BUDGET

1. Projected Annual Gross Sales

When entrepreneurs get ready to create advertising budgets for their businesses, it's important to take projected annual gross sales into account. This method helps shield entrepreneurs from spending too much or too little on advertising. It is recommended to calculate your minimum and maximum advertising budget figures by 10 percent and 12 percent of your projected annual gross sales. Then, expand each figure by the markup you make on your average sales transaction. This figure can differ year to year depending on both your company's performance and your product markups.

2. Marketing Objectives

Marketing objectives differ across organizations and can greatly affect what appears on a company's advertising budget. Determine which marketing objective will assist you to reach your annual business goals. Marketing objectives might comprise of obtaining 5 percent more repetitive customers, experiencing growth each month or increasing annual sales by 10 percent. The objectives you come up with help you define marketing strategies and tactics, which ultimately give insight into how and where you advertise, both of which are things that can affect the advertising budget.

3. Time of Year

Advertising pricing may change during different times over the year, such as a new season or during popular holidays. While some advertisers may offer discounts, others may increase their prices if they feel their readership or viewership may peak during specific times or events. If you're trying to position an advertisement in a magazine's most popular issue of the year or a television commercial during a highly televised event, such as the Super Bowl, you can expect a change in the amount you spend to promote your product or service.

4. Product Launch vs. Existing Product

If you're introducing a new product to the market, consider this factor as you create your advertising budget, as it affects how much you spend. When products are launched, business owners often go into overdrive coming up with diverse ways to advertise and promote their new product or service to potential clients. This may generate an advertising budget to be higher than it would be for a product that customers are already aware of and have purchased in the past.

5. Budgeting Method

Customers tastes vary with time and so do the trends. Thus, keeping an eye on those changing trends and putting forward a method that counters those changes by changing the advertising means can pay off later next time. Once, the advertisers get the feel of how to intercept the changes, they will be able to make use of advertising means properly, which will bring down the budget needed for advertisements to bring the same number of buyers or even more with the same budget level.

Among all the methods, the percentage-of-sales method is the most common one and involves setting up a percentage of about 3-5% of the revenue of the current year as the budget for the next year. This means the fluctuations in the number of sales will surely alter the budget.

6. Affordability

It is quite natural for a small company that is able to generate ₹ 50, 00,000 on yearly basis to be able to afford a smaller advertising budget as compared to large multi-national companies with revenue in billions. Large companies may not find it difficult to run international campaigns for the promotion of their products. On the other hand, for smaller businesses, allocating ₹ 40,000 – ₹90, 000 for promotional purpose every year is really huge amount to spend and is a difficult task to manage.

7. Organizational Characteristics

There are several factors regarding the organizational characteristics that are to be considered. These factors vary from one organization to another as their characteristics differ and influence the advertising expenditure.

- Structure of the organization i.e., centralized, decentralized, and balanced, formalization and complexity of the organization.
- Power and politics in the organization with vested interests.
- The use of expert opinion e.g., consultants.
- Characteristics of the decision maker (Preference, experience, expertise etc.).
- Approval and negotiation channels
- Pressure on senior managers to arrive at the optional budget.

ECONOMIC ANALYSIS IN SETTING AND ALLOCATING BUDGETS

When a company decides how much to spend on advertising, they use a theory called economic marginal analysis. In simple terms, they keep adding money to their advertising budget for a specific type of advertising as long as the extra money they spend brings in more additional sales revenue than it costs.For instance, if a company sells products that have been around for a while and they notice that they are making more money from each customer, they should increase their advertising budget. This includes both advertising and sales calls made by their salespeople.

On the flip side, if a lot of other companies are also spending a ton of money on advertising in the same area, it might not be as effective, so the company should decrease their advertising budget.This same idea can be used for other parts of marketing, like promotions, sales calls, distribution, and pricing. By analyzing all these components, a company can figure out the best amount to spend on each to get the most value for their money.

MARKET EXPERIMENATTAION AND BUDGETING

One effective method to figure out how advertising impacts sales is by conducting real-world market experiments. In these experiments, companies deliberately and carefully change their advertising spending levels in different geographic areas. They then closely observe how these changes affect sales over a period, which can sometimes span several years.For instance, a company might decide to spend more on advertising in one city while keeping advertising levels the same in another. By tracking sales data in both locations, they can draw insights into the relationship between advertising investment and sales performance.

For example: Let's consider a recent example to illustrate this concept. Imagine a global fast-food chain wants to assess the impact of a new advertising campaign promoting a new burger. They decide to allocate a higher advertising budget to certain regions of the country, while maintaining a standard budget in others.Over the course of a year, they closely monitor burger sales in both the high-advertising and standard-advertising regions. By analyzing the data, they can determine if the increased advertising spending led to a significant boost in burger sales. This information helps them fine-tune their advertising budget allocation for future campaigns, ensuring they get the best return on their investment.

In essence, market experimentation and budgeting are practical ways for companies to make informed decisions about how much to invest in advertising and where to allocate those resources for optimal sales results.

REGRESSION ANALYSIS FOR BUDGETING

Another approach to estimating the relationship between advertising and sales—the advertising-response curve—is to look at the historical patterns of sales and advertising. When advertising changed in the past, what happened to sales? Or if the advertising level differed in different sales areas or by different advertising media, how did sales differ? Such an approach is relatively inexpensive, as it uses in hand.

This approach is cost-effective because it relies on historical data that a company already has on hand.

To analyze these patterns systematically, a statistical technique called multiple regression analysis is often used. In this analysis, a model is created to predict sales in one time period based on various factors, including:

- Sales in the previous period.
- Advertising spending in the current period.
- Advertising spending in the previous period.
- Advertising spending two periods back.
- Other marketing factors, like distribution and pricing, as well as the presence of competing brands.
- Some measure of how effective the advertising message is.
- Data on what competitors are doing with their advertising.

By using this approach, businesses can gain insights into how different factors, including advertising, influence their sales over time.

IMPORTANT QUESTIONS

1. What do you understand by advertising budget? Discuss the factors affecting advertising budget.
2. What do you understand by advertising appropriations? Explain in detail different methods of advertising appropriations.
3. What do you understand by:
   (a) Experimental approach
   (b) Regression analysis
   (c) Marginal economic analysis

❍ ❍ ❍

Chapter 14

MEDIA TACTICS

INTRODUCTION

The Global age is the age of information and communication. In this aggressive competitive world, where information and proactive action or decision determines the fate of a company, product, person or system, it becomes necessary to be informed and knowledgeable. Media works as a platform to exchange information, knowledge and make consumers aware of the market information. Therefore, media acts as a catalyst, transformer to diffuse, which filters and collects response about all events thus, spreading awareness.

DEFINITION

"Advertising media is defined as the media channels through which advertising messages are communicated to the existing and prospective customers by the advertisers."

Advertising media plays a crucial role in business and marketing for organizations. There are many organizations who offer products and services in the same product class to the same customers. But, it is unlikely for every customer to know about every brand in the market. This is why organizations use advertising media to reach its customers. This helps to create a buzz about the brand, thus, building a strong brand.

TYPES OF ADVERTISING MEDIA

Advertising media is an important domain for any and all the organizations. Overtime, ads are being showcased and communicated to customers through several ways. There are different types of advertising media used. Depending upon various variables like budget, reach, past performance, customer preferences and the like, companies choose the required advertising media which helps in boosting sales of the brand. Advertising media is of following types:

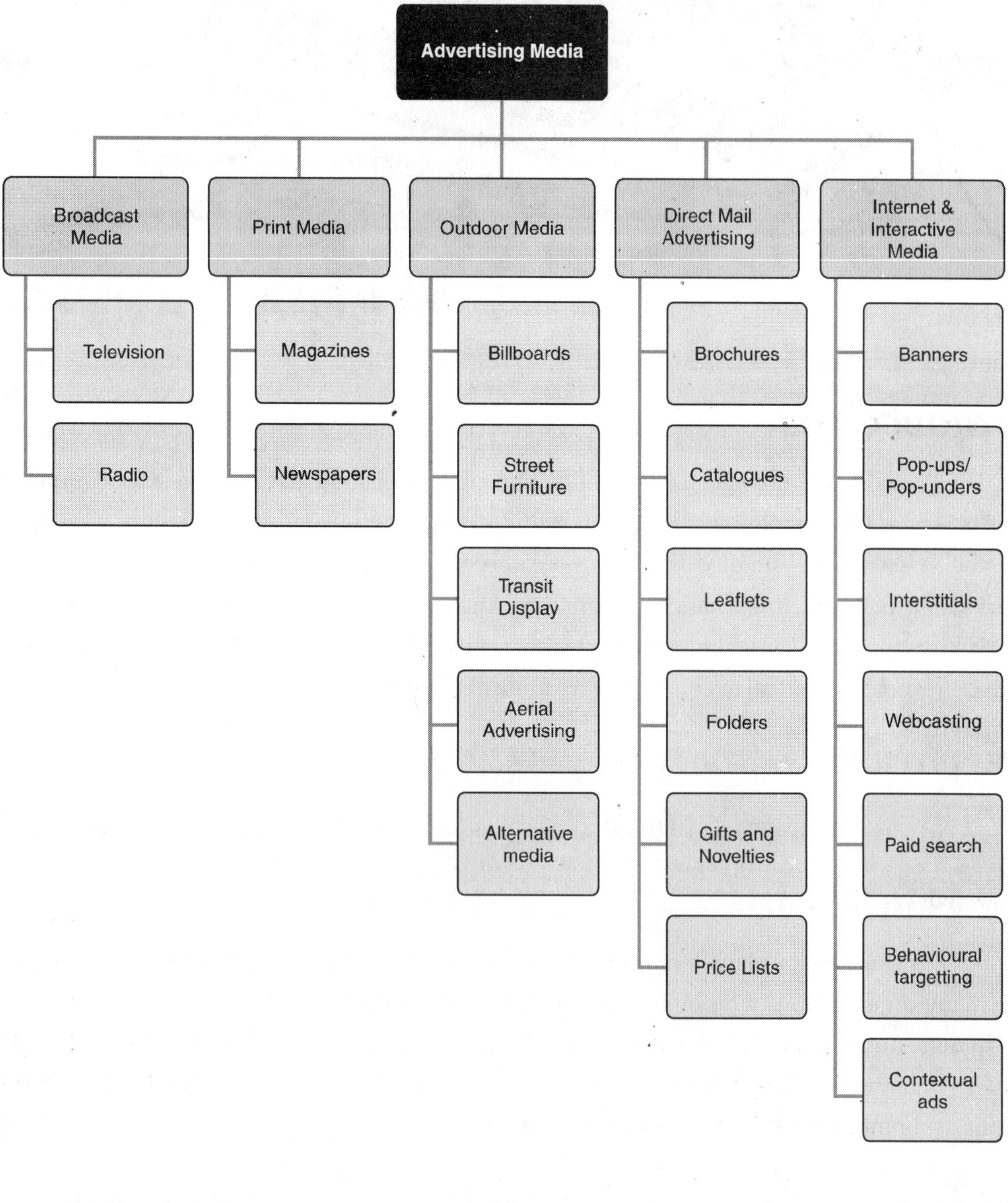

1. BROADCAST MEDIA

TELEVISION

Television is the ideal advertising medium as its ability to combine sound, image, color, motion and emotion presents the advertiser with the opportunity to develop most creative and effective appeals. It gives the product a "larger than life" image which provides an edge to the organization over its competitors. Even small companies with limited budgets benefit from this media as it gives an impression of "big" companies to customers who have their own advertising spots. It is the best place for an advertiser to place his/her advertisements for best reach. Despite a growing spectrum of options people find more information from televisions than all the other sources combined. This is the reason why it is considered as one of the most credible sources of information. TV has numerous advantages as well as disadvantages as listed below:

ADVANTAGES	DISADVANTAGES
Creativity and Impact The interaction of sight and sound offers a great opportunity for presenting the advertising message creatively, dramatically and with life like representations of products and services.	**Costs** Even though per person cost of advertising is low, the expense of buying airtime and cost of producing a commercial is quite high.
Coverage and Cost Effectiveness TV is a popular medium among companies selling mass- consumption products as it lets them reach mass markets cost effectively.	**Low Selectivity** Advertisers who are seeking a very specific, often small, target audience find the coverage extending beyond their market, reducing its cost effectiveness.
Captivity and Attention TV ads have an impact on customers through heavy repetition and exposure to catchy slogans and jingles.	**Fleeting Message** Television commercials usually last for 30 seconds or less and leave nothing substantial for the viewer to consider or examine.
Selectivity and Flexibility Advertisers usually adjust their marketing strategies to take advantage of different geographical markets through local or spot ads in specific market areas.	**Limited Viewer Attention** Getting consumer's attention during commercial break is challenging because of: • **Zipping:** fast forward through ads • **Zapping:** changing channels to avoid ads • **Gracing:** scanning list of channels for something interesting to watch

EXAMPLE: DABUR VATIKA- BRAVE AND BEAUTIFUL

Vatika is one of the power brands of Dabur and the hair oil and shampoo brand astonished the world by broadcasting an advertisement showing a young mother- a cancer survivor who is trying to get her life back to normal against challenging circumstances. Through this gesture, Dabur Vatika tries to emphasize the philosophy that "some people do not need hair to look beautiful". The brand encouraged cancer survivors all over the country to share their experiences to inspire others. The brand carved out a niche to differentiate itself from the other brands and it also sends strong signals to the audience about the notion of beauty.

Thus, television is a great medium for generating awareness and altering the customer's perception, as customers do not only buy brand's product but also, the idea for which the brand stands for.

RADIO

Television has been considered an ideal advertising medium, and to many, it epitomizes the glamour and excitement of the industry. But over the years, radio has evolved as a local advertising medium and has become pervasive. Radio at present covers 97.5% of the total population and 91% of total area of India. Radio has survived and flourished as an advertising medium which plays an integral role in the lifestyles of consumers as it has power to reach and influence their purchase behaviour. Radio has many advantages as well as disadvantages over other media:

ADVANTAGES	DISADVANTAGES
Cost and Efficiency Radio commercials are inexpensive as they require only a script or a pre-recorded message to be broadcasted by the station. The low cost also means that the advertiser can build more reach and frequency by using different radio stations.	**Creative Limitations** The radio advertiser cannot show the product, demonstrate it or use any type of visual appeal for creating awareness.
Receptivity Consumers have an emotional connection with the radio as compared to other media as they perceive radio as more personally relevant to them.	**Fragmentation** Due to large number of stations, the percentage of audience tuned to a particular station is small and fragmented.

Selectivity Radio lets organizations focus their advertising on specialized audiences such as certain demographic and lifestyle groups. Moreover, it can reach those audiences that media can't.	**Chaotic Buying Procedure** The media planning and purchase procedure becomes chaotic if the advertiser wishes to use nationwide advertising radio spots.
Flexibility The advertisers can change their message before it goes on air which provides more flexibility.	**Limited Research Data** Most radio stations are small and lack revenue for detailed studies of their audiences.
Mental Imagery While creative options for radio are limited, advertisers take advantage of absence of visual imagery to encourage the listeners to use their imagination when processing a message.	**Limited Listener Attention** It is challenging to retain listener's attention during commercials as radio programming, mostly music, is a background to some other activity.
Integrated Marketing Opportunities To provide synergistic effects, it can be combined with newspapers, television, and magazines to generate awareness and communicate the message.	**Competition from Digital Media** Digital based technologies like satellites radio and podcasts are impacting the listening audience for commercial radio.

EXAMPLE: WHATSAPP: TACKLING FAKE NEWS

In a bid to control spreading of fake new, Whatsapp, the Facebook owned company, rolled out radio campaigns across various Indian states, asking people to check the authenticity of the messages before sharing it with others. This also encourages the users to report the content which they might consider inflammatory. The radio campaign was aired across 46 Hindi speaking stations of All India Radio.

Thus, radio advertising helps to provide information and creating awareness about a product or service at lower cost as compared to other mediums.

2. PRINT MEDIA

MAGAZINES

Over the past decades magazines have grown rapidly to serve the informational, educational and entertainment needs of wide range of readers in business as well as consumer markets. It is the most specialized of all advertising media as it is designed to appeal to nearly every type of consumer in terms of demographics, activities, interest or fascination. A wide variety makes magazines an appealing medium to a vast number of advertisers. Magazines have a long advertising life, lasting beyond the immediate issue because subscribers read and reread them. Various advantages and disadvantages of magazines are highlighted below:

ADVANTAGES	DISADVANTAGES
Selectivity Magazines provide advertisers with demographic and geographical selectivity as they are published for special interest groups.	**Costs** The costs vary according to the size of audience, their reach, selectivity and the services offered.
Reproduction Quality The reproduction quality is far superior as compared to other mediums as magazines are printed on high quality papers and it provides excellent reproduction in white, black or color.	**Limited Reach and Frequency** Since a wide range of magazines are weekly or monthly publications, the opportunity for building frequency through the use of same publications is limited.
Creative Flexibility Magazines offer advertisers a lot of flexibility in terms of type, size, and placement and also offer (at an extra charge) special options that can enhance the creativity of the advertisement.	**Long Lead Time** Major publications have a 30-day or 60-day lead time, which means the space must be purchased and the ad must be prepared well in advance of actual publication date.
Permanence Magazines are read over several days and are often kept for reference. Readers are also, exposed to ads on multiple occasions and may also pass the magazines along to other readers.	**Clutter and Competition** The more successful a magazine becomes more advertising pages it attracts and this leads to clutter and also, competition amongst the companies.
Prestige It portrays a favorable image of the company. Companies whose products rely heavily on perceived quality, reputation, and/or image, often buy space in prestigious publications with high quality editorial content	
Consumer Receptivity and Engagement Consumers are more receptive to advertising in magazines as they are generally purchased because the information they contain, interests the readers and ads provide additional information that are necessary in purchase decision.	

Services Magazines conduct research studies on consumers dealing with consumer trends, changing purchase patterns, media usage and the like.	

EXAMPLE: HYUNDAI

Extravagant special effects are great attention grabbers. A creatively designed print ad with innovative typography makes great use of that fact. This innovative ad clearly states that the Hyundai is designed by keeping human needs in mind.

NEWSPAPERS

Newspapers are the second major form of print media and are an especially important medium of advertising for local advertisers as well as national advertisers. Newspaper advertisers receive cumulative discounts for buying large column inches over one- month, three-month, and a yearlong period. Readers rely on information in newspapers which gives them high credibility. Newspaper readers also pay enough attention to the articles they read and also tend to pay more attention on the advertisements. Many consumers rely on newspaper advertisements for grocery shopping other similar discounts. Like all other media, newspaper has advantages as well as disadvantages:

ADVANTAGES	DISADVANTAGES
Extensive Penetration In most areas, 50 percent or more households read the newspaper and this number can reach up to 70 percent among households with high income and education levels, thus ensuring extensive market penetration.	**Poor Reproduction** The coarse paper stock and absence of color contributes to poor reproduction quality of newspapers. Even though high-quality newspapers are available, they are costly which is not desirable to many advertisers.
Flexibility Although closing time for special or Sunday advertisement is longer, the closing time for daily advertising is usually 24 hours before publishing providing more flexibility in terms of writing, format and creativity.	**Short Life Span** A daily newspaper ad is unlikely to have an impact beyond the day of publication as it is kept for less than a day and repeat exposure is highly unlikely.
Geographic Selectivity Newspapers generally offer more geographic and territorial selectivity as advertisers can choose a paper or a combination of papers that reaches the area with greatest sales potential.	**Lack Of Selectivity** Most newspapers reach broad and very diverse group of consumers which makes it difficult for marketers to focus on narrowly defined market segments.
Reader Involvement and Acceptance Most consumers rely on newspaper for information, entertainment and assistance with consumption decisions.	**Clutter** As more than 60 percent of newspapers are devoted to advertisements, the advertiser's message must compete with numerous other ads for consumer's attention and interest.
Services Offered Newspapers offer merchandising services and programs, art services and copywriting. They are also excellent sources of market information through knowledge of market knowledge and extensive research.	

EXAMPLE: ADVERTISMENT OF E-COMMERCE GIANTS

3. OUTDOOR MEDIA

Outdoor advertising is the oldest established form of advertising, evidence of its use has been found on Greek and Roman remains. Earlier outdoor advertising was mainly concerned with tobacco and alcohol, but this has changed over the past decades. It is a pervasive form of communication if one lives in urban or suburban area. The major reason for continuous use of outdoor advertising is the ability to remain innovative through technology. Outdoor advertising encompasses many advertising forms:

(a) **Billboards :** Billboard advertisements can be large and spectacular making them major attention getting devices. Billboard's large size gives the impression that the product and message are important. They also help to communicate a firm's location to travelers. These consist of:

- Bulletins
- Wall murals
- Posters

(b) **Street Furniture :** This consists of advertisements on bus shelters, urban furniture, kiosks, convenience stores and shopping malls, to grab the attention of the audience.

(c) **Transit advertising :** Transit advertising is targeted at millions of people who are exposed to commercial transportation facilities and includes buses, airports, truck sides, taxi displays, wrapped vehicles, commuter trains and subways.

(d) **Aerial Advertising :** Airplanes pulling banners, skywriting (letters as high as 1200 feet) and blimps (pompous representations); all constitute aerial advertising. These Medias are not expensive in absolute terms and can be useful for reaching specific target markets.

(e) **Alternative Media :** This consists of advertising through Arenas and Stadiums, Campuses, Resorts, Digital media and Cinema to attract the attention of the audiences towards the product offerings.

ADVANTAGES	DISADVANTAGES
Wide Coverage Broad exposure is possible through proper placement of advertisements.	**Waste coverage** It is not likely that everyone passing a billboard is the target audience leading to waste coverage.
Frequency Purchase cycles are of 30 day periods, consumers are exposed a number of times ensuring extensive coverage.	**Cost** Because of decreasing signage available and high cost associated with inflatables, outdoor advertising can be very expensive.
Geographic Flexibility Outdoor advertising can be done along highways, near stores, or on billboards, almost anywhere the law permits.	**Image problems** Outdoor advertising suffers disregard from some customers.
Creativity Large print, color, layout, can be used to enhance creativity and this helps in attracting the attention of the audience.	**Wear out** Because of high frequency of exposures, outdoor ads may lead to a quick wear out. People are likely to get tired of watching the same ad daily.
Timeliness Many outdoor ads appear in or near shopping areas or on or in the vehicles taking customers there, thus resulting in timely exposures.	

EXAMPLE: AMAZON AND OLA

Amazon's #AurDikhao campaign to apprise the customers about the variety of products available on amazon and Ola's a perfect to use the grab handles in a bus as a perfect reminder to take Ola auto, for every time when you stand in a crowded bus.

4. DIRECT MAIL ADVERTISING MEDIA

While many companies rely on a variety of promotional mix elements to move their products through intermediaries, a growing number of companies are going directly to consumers. These companies believe that while promotional mix elements help in creating brand image, generating awareness, conveying information, going directly to the customer can generate an immediate response. This response can take the form of an inquiry, a purchase or a vote. This includes:

- Catalogues
- Brochures
- Leaflets
- Folders
- Gifts and novelties
- Price lists

The various advantages and disadvantages are listed below:

ADVANTAGES	DISADVANTAGES
Selective Reach It helps to reach a large audience and eliminates waste coverage.	**Rising Costs** If postal rates and printing costs increase, it drives up the overall cost of direct mail advertising.
Segmentation Marketers can purchase lists of recent product purchasers, car buyers, bank card holders which allow them to segment the target market geographically, demographically and so on.	**Accuracy** One of the advantages of direct mail is that it targets the potential customers, and for this the marketers rely on the customers lists. However, if the lists are not updated, they may be give inaccurate results.

Personalization and Flexibility No other medium allows the marketers to personalize the message which provides it with more flexibility.	Image factors It is found irritating by many customers and is generally referred to as junk or spam mail. This reduces the impact of direct advertising even if it is done by established companies like GM.
Costs While costs involved in direct mail are very high but its ability to specifically target the audience eliminates waste coverage.	
Measures Of Effectiveness No other medium can measure its advertising efforts as well as direct advertising.	

EXAMPLE: EARTH HOUR CAMPAIGN

Designed as a direct mail campaign by WWF to raise awareness about the amount of energy that we waste when we leave our lights on overnight, The Earth Hour Candle Box was a triumph of direct mail. As the candle was pulled out of the box, its design allowed it to simulate lights being switched off. The uniquely packaged candles were sent to CEOs and business leaders.

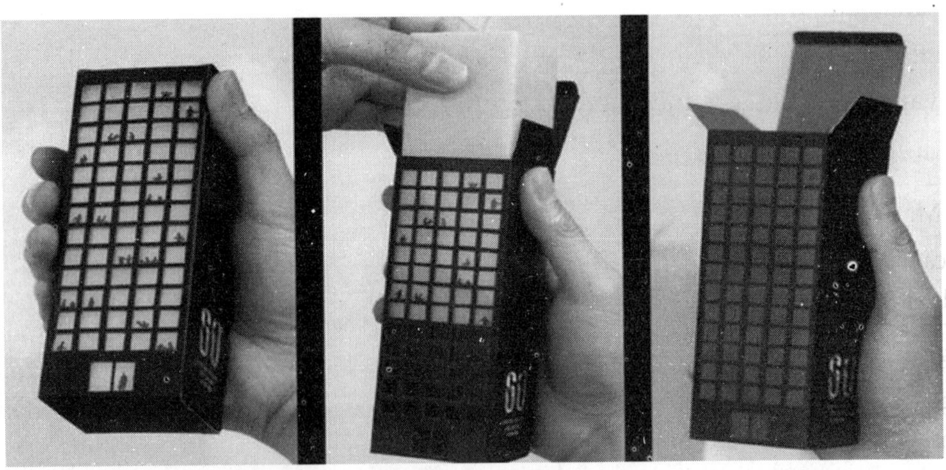

5. INTERNET AND INTERACTIVE MEDIA

The Internet is an advertising medium just like broadcast and print media. Companies and organizations working to promote their products and services must consider this medium just like they would consider any other medium like newspapers, magazines, television and so on. Internet advertising employs a variety of media as listed below:

(a) **Banners :** Banner ads are the most common form of advertising which may be used for creating awareness or entering viewers into contests and sweepstakes. They create a favorable attitude towards the ads through repetitive exposure.

(b) **Pop-Ups or Pop-Unders :** Sometimes a window or a character appears on the window screen while surfing the internet to catch your attention. These are known as pop-ups. The ads that appear underneath a webpage and become visible only when the user leaves the site are known as pop-unders. Many marketers believe that they are in their decline stage as their frequency and effectiveness has reduced due to availability of pop-up screeners.

(c) **Interstitials :** These are the ads that appear on the screen when the user waits for a site's content to download. However, these can also be blocked by pop-up blockers.

(d) **Push Technologies or Webcasting Technologies :** These may have webpages and news updates which allow companies to push the message to consumers rather than waiting for them to find it.

(e) **Paid Search :** Commonly known as Search Engine Advertising in which the advertisers pay only when a consumer clicks on their ads or links them from a search engine page.

(f) **Behavioural Targeting :** This involves targeting customers based on their website surfing behaviour. By using internet protocol and clickstream data, buyers can be identified, and ads be targeted to them.

(g) **Contextual Ads :** Advertisers target the ads based on content of the web page like an advertiser may place airline ad on travel site and a golf club ad in golf site.

The various advantages and disadvantages related to Internet marketing are:

ADVANTAGES	DISADVANTAGES
Target Marketing Web can target very specific groups of individuals with minimum of waste coverage.	**Privacy** Internet marketers must be careful not to invade upon the privacy of users.
Message Tailoring Messages can be designed to appeal the specific needs and wants of the target audience.	**Annoyance** Having to install an additional software, difficulty in navigation, has led customers to permanently leave sites.
Interactive Capabilities It provides strong potential for increasing customer involvement and satisfaction and immediate feedback for buyers and sellers.	**Potential for Deception** Data collection without customer's knowledge, hacking, credit card theft are among the problems customers face while surfing the internet.

Creativity Creatively designed sites can enhance the company's image, leading to repeat visits and positively positioning the company in consumer's mind.	**Measurement Problems** A quick review of forecasts, audience profiles, and other research statistics offered by research providers demonstrates a great deal f variance leading to lack of reliability and validity.
Speed Internet is the quickest means of acquiring information related to products and services offered by the organizations.	

EXAMPLE: MYNTRA

Established as a website to sell personalized gift items, Myntra today is India's largest fashion and lifestyle e-commerce store that serves millions of fashion enthusiasts every day. With the onset of smartphones and rapidly increasing product sales, building a mobile presence seemed like a natural next step. With its web store predominantly depending on showcasing rich visual content, videos and images, Myntra aimed to keep up with the evolving market. The new design allowed for easy viewing of multiple options on the same page. All images, once loaded, remained and adjusted their quality according to the device. This made Myntra as India's first mobile shopping experience with an 80% shift in sales from desktop.

FACTORS AFFECTING CHOICE OF ADVERTISING MEDIA

1. **The media mix :** Many alternatives for media and media vehicles are available to advertisers. So, to choose one or more mediums to create a voice of a brand involves considering factors like communication objectives, characteristics of products and

services, size of budget, individual preferences and the like. If a product needs to be demonstrated, then television is a more suitable medium and if awareness about coupons or offers is to be generated, then, internet or direct mail advertising are more suitable mediums.

2. **Target market coverage :** The goal of media planner is to extend media coverage to as many members of target audience as possible while eliminating the amount of waste coverage. If wide coverage is required then broadcast media should be preferred. If selective media advertising is required, then direct mail advertising is preferred by advertisers.

3. **Nature of the competition :** The nature of the competition deploys greater influence on the selection of the media. If the competition is stiff, utmost care is needed in the selection of medium and a larger advertising budget is also required.

4. **Reputation of the medium :** Newspapers and magazines offer a beautiful illustration for the product. There are a few newspapers and magazines having an international reputation with a high readership. Advertisements in such magazines and newspapers are generally recognized and believed as true. Such advertisements also add prestige to the product.

5. **Cost of the media :** The cost of the medium is an important factor in the selection of the media. Advertisements in certain media are expensive like broadcast advertisements. Print advertisements are generally considered less expensive. Yet, certain magazines and newspapers, having larger circulation and high reputation charge higher rates. The rates also differ depending upon the space occupied and the preferential positions. The first page of a newspaper is rarely missed by the reader. Hence, they have more attention value, than the advertisements presented anywhere inside the newspaper.

6. **The nature of product :** A product that is needed by all will encourage mass media like print, broadcast, outdoor and the like. A product needing demonstration requires television and internet advertising. Industrial products find favor of print media than broadcast media. Also, products like cigarettes and alcohol are never advertised on radio and television.

7. **The budget available :** A manufacturer may be dreaming of advertising on national television and films and may have a bold and very colorful plan of advertising. However, if budget is not allowed, then he must use low budget media like his newspaper and outdoor advertising. Instead of color print in magazines, he may be forced to go in for black and white. Thus, the resource constraints decide the media choice.

MEDIA PLANNING

Some of the basic terms and concepts used in media planning are enlisted below:

Media planning

Media planning is a process involving a series of decisions to deliver the promotional message to the prospective purchasers and end-users of the product. These decisions may be altered as the plan develops. Media planning is the best way to determine how to get an advertiser's message across the target market. The goal of media planning is to find the best combination of different mediums to communicate the message to existing and potential customers at lower cost.

Medium

The general classification of delivery systems includes broadcast media, print media, internet, and outdoor advertising.

Reach

It is a measure to determine the number of different audience members exposed at least once to a media vehicle in eachperiod.

Coverage

It refers to the potential audience that receives the message through a medium. The difference between coverage and reach is that coverage is related to potential audience while reach refers to actual audience.

Frequency

The number of times a receiver is exposed to the message through a medium in a specified time.

DEVELOPING A MEDIA PLAN

The media plan specifically focuses on how a message can be delivered through different mediums. This involves a series of stages are highlighted below:

1. MARKET ANALYSIS

In developing a media plan, market analysis is carried out although the focus is on media and delivering the message. It involves detailed analysis of external and internal environment, marketing plan and creative plan.

(a) **The Situation Analysis :** The intention of performing situation analysis is to understand the marketing problem by analyzing the company and its competitors based on:

- Size and share of total market
- Sales history, costs, profits
- Distribution practices
- Identification of prospects
- Nature of product

(b) **The marketing strategy plan :** It focuses on planning activities that would solve marketing problems like setting marketing objectives, budget strategy, distribution strategy, identifying the target audience and the like.

(c) **The creative strategy plan :** Creative without strategy is called 'Art.' Creative with strategy is called 'Advertising.' The purpose of developing a creative strategy is to communicate one voice of the brand to the target audience and involves determination of:

- Brand positioning
- Copy themes
- Number and sizes of advertisements
- Customer targeting and customer satisfaction

2. SETTING MEDIA OBJECTIVES

Media objectives are designed to lead to the attainment of communications and marketing objectives. Media objectives are the goals for media program and can be accomplished through media strategies.

Example: Create awareness through:

- broadcast media to provide 80% coverage in target market
- Concentrate on heavy advertising in summers and light advertising in fall.

3. DEVELOPING AND IMPLEMENTING MEDIA STRATEGIES

After developing the media objectives, media planners need to establish a strategy in order to accomplish them. It involves the following criteria:

(a) **The media mix :** It is not necessary that only one medium be used for creating awareness among the target audience. A combination of two or more Medias can also be used. This depends on various factors like characteristics of product or service, budget considerations, preferences of the target market etc. By using media mix, media planners can add more versatility to their strategies, and this can also enhance their coverage, reach and frequency levels.

(b) Target market coverage : The media planner decides which target market should receive the most media emphasis. The most optimistic, although unrealistic scenario is when there is full market coverage. More realistically, either the media coverage does not envelope the entire market or the media coverage exceeds the target market leading to over exposure i.e. waste coverage. Thus, it is the task of media planner to extend the media coverage to as many members of target audience while reducing the waste coverage.

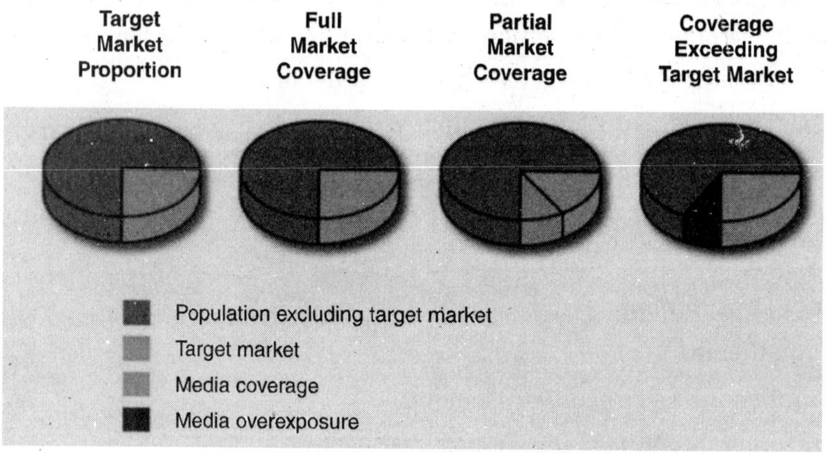

(c) Scheduling : Companies like to keep their advertising in front of the customers as a constant reminder of the product and brand name. Thus, the main objective of scheduling is to combine the highest potential buying time to the promotional efforts of the organization. There are 3 scheduling methods available to a media planner:

– **Continuity :** It refers to a continuous pattern of advertising which usually means every day, every week or every month. Such strategies are used for food products, laundry detergents, or other products consumed on an ongoing basis without any regard to seasonality.

ADVANTAGES	DISADVANTAGES
Serves as a constant reminder to the customer	Higher costs
Covers the entire customer decision making and purchasing cycle	Potential for waste coverage
Provides complete information like price, offers available, locations etc.	

– **Flighting :** This uses a less regular schedule with intermittent periods of advertising and non-advertising. At some time periods there are heavy promotional expenditures and at other times, there may be no advertising. Many banks spend no money on advertising during summers but maintain advertising for the rest of the year.

ADVANTAGES	DISADVANTAGES
Cost efficiency as advertising is done during purchase cycles.	Increased possibility of wear out
Allows for using media mix efficiently due to limited budgets.	Lack of awareness and retention of promotional message during non-scheduled time
	Vulnerable to competitors' efforts during the lean advertising period

– **Pulsing :** It is a combination of the first two methods. In this, the continuity is maintained but at certain time periods, the promotional efforts are increased. This is used by deodorant selling companies, as the products are used for the entire year but more during the summers.

ADVANTAGES	DISADVANTAGES
Covers different market situations	Higher costs
Serves as a constant reminder	Not applicable for seasonal products

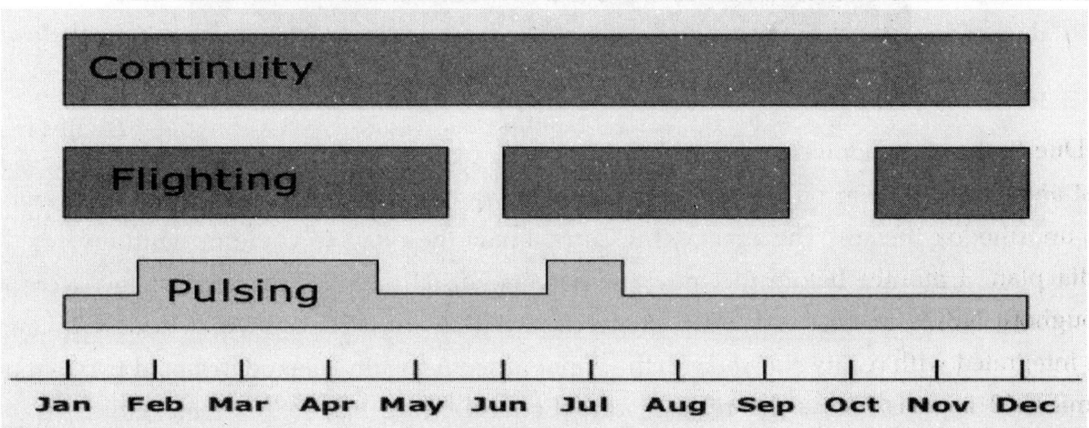

(d) Flexibility : Due to the changing marketing environment, strategies need to be modified according to the marketing opportunities, threats, availability of media or changes in media vehicles. If a media plan does not have enough flexibility, then, the company may not be able to address new threats.

(e) **Budget considerations :** This is one of the most crucial decisions when developing media strategy. The media planner tries to come up with an optimal strategy that communicates the promotional message to the customers at least cost and reduced waste coverage.

4. EVALUATION AND FOLLOW UP

Having implemented the strategies, the media planner needs to know whether they were successful. And if the strategies were successful the future need to be identified and if unsuccessful, then shortcomings to be analyzed.

CASE STUDY: THE DA VINCI CODE- MEDIA PLAN OF THE YEAR

Due to the stupendous success of Dan Brown's novel, its movie adaptation was one of the most anticipated movies of the past decade. But it was based on one of the most controversial and unorthodox themes. The agency, MCCann, knew they had to come up with an infallible media plan. 3 months before the movie was released, 60- second TV commercials were run throughout NBC's telecast of Winter Olympics. A successful "The Da Vinci Code Challenge" was integrated with reality shows, with the winners acquiring an all-expenses-paid trip to movie premiere. 2 months before the release, outdoor advertising helped to create more hype. In addition to this, the agency tied up with Google and TiVo to participate in games and contests to solve the Da Vinci Mysteries.

As a result of a $25 million campaign, the movie was a great success. An exit poll disclosed that 40% of the opening weekend audience was aware of the marketing campaign of the movie.

IMPORTANT QUESTIONS

1. What do you understand by advertising media? Discuss its importance and the factors affecting advertising media?
2. What are the different modes of advertising under
   (a) Broadcast Media
   (b) Print Media
   (c) Outdoor Media
   (d) Direct Mail Advertising
   (e) Internet and Interactive Advertising
3. What do you mean by advertising media? Explain important types of advertising media.
4. Explain the various steps involved in the process of media planning and scheduling.
5. What are the various media strategies involved while media planning?

❍ ❍ ❍